Tragedy of Fraud - Insider Trading Edition

The fall from Big 4 audit partner to prison inmate

Dedication

This book is dedicated to

my beloved wife, Beth,
for her encouragement and patience because
with her support and love I am living life to the full
and achieved my dream of
running my own CPA firm and becoming a writer

and

my parents, James and Betty Ulvog,
in appreciation for their love
and encouragement for all these years.

Tragedy of Fraud - Insider Trading Edition

The fall from Big 4 audit partner to prison inmate

James L. Ulvog, CPA

Riverstone Finance Press
Alta Loma, California

www.riverstonefinancepress.com

Tragedy of Fraud - Insider Trading Edition

The fall from Big 4 audit partner to prison inmate

The text in this book is a compilation of posts previously published in the author's weblog, Attestation Update (attestationupdate.com). The posts have been edited from when they originally appeared.

This book is distributed with the understanding that the author and publisher are not rendering accounting or other professional services in this publication. If accounting advice or expert assistance is required, the services of a competent professional should be retained.

Published by:
Riverstone Finance Press
8780 19th St. #305
Alta Loma, CA 91701

riverstonefinancepress.com

Cover design by Caligraphics. http://caligraphics.net

ISBN-13: 978-1-942066-00-2

Contents

The long fall

Scott London, a respected CPA and a senior level partner in a prestigious accounting firm, stands in front of a federal judge this lovely Thursday morning, the 21st of April, 2014. Restraining his emotions as much as possible, he listens as the judge sentences him to fourteen months in federal prison.

A year in jail.

He lost his CPA license the previous December. Lost his lucrative job when he got fired a year earlier. His reputation and good name have been shredded many times over along the way.

Why is he here?

He pled guilty to one felony.

What did he do?

Pass confidential information on to a golf buddy, who traded on the inside information, and got paid several wads of cash and some jewelry for his effort.

How far is up?

He was an audit partner in a major international CPA firm in one of the largest markets in the world.

He worked in the Los Angeles office of KPMG. Some of you may remember the name Peat, Marwick, Mitchell. He was in charge of the audit practice, not just for that office but for the entire southwest region of the U.S. Fifty other partners reported to him. About 500 auditors worked in his area of responsibility.

Published reports suggest his salary was $900,000 a year. Assuming he actually got away for two weeks a year, that would be $18,000 a week. At that level you don't work five days a week. He was making about $3,000 each day of his six day weeks.

He later claimed in an interview he was making less than that, about $650,000 a year. For six day work weeks over 50 weeks a year, that is still about $2,200 a day.

That compensation may be trivial compared to the sports or entertainment world, but that's a level that every other accountant can only dream about.

He had respect. Responsibility. Authority. Recognized expertise.

He had another decade to enjoy the peak of his profession.

The dream job.

But that was a year ago.

How far is down?

He's now a convicted felon. On his way to prison. He confessed to fourteen incidents of insider trading.

He will likely never work in a financial job again.

Remember that 'How would this look on the front page of the Wall Street Journal?' test that is bandied about as a measure of whether something is right or wrong?

He has seen his photograph on the front page of the WSJ. Above the fold.

In color.

Photos are courtesy of the FBI, taken during their surveillance of him. Those photos show him the moment a bundle of cash was passed to him. In broad daylight. In a parking lot.

On July 18, 2014, Scott London checked in to the Taft Correctional Institute, which is about 45 miles southwest of Bakersfield, California. His sentence is 14 months, with expected release about two months earlier than his full sentence.

From the partner with ultimate decision authority over work of 500 professionals to a prison inmate. That is a long fall.

Why did he do it?

We don't know.

What did he do? What will it cost him?

That is the story told in the pages that follow.

Full disclosure

For about three years, I worked in the Albuquerque office of Peat, Marwick, Mitchell. That was the name of the firm prior to a merger than produced KPMG. The P and M in the current name came from Peat and Marwick. I had and still have the utmost respect for the people I worked with back then.

I am intentionally a one person CPA firm providing audits and reviews to the nonprofit community. That makes me a sub-microscopically insignificant competitor to KPMG. My total billable hours since starting my own firm are dramatically less than the number of people that work for KPMG.

Filter my comments as you wish.

I included this disclosure in many of the posts. I decided not to remove those redundant comments from this book in order to retain the feel of the story as it developed.

About this book

The book you are reading consists of articles that were originally published as a series of posts on my blog, Attestation Update (www.attestationupdate.com).

Editing - The posts have been slightly edited. Some redundant comments were removed. There is some light editing - grammar fixed, unneeded introductions pulled, links to the subsequent post removed.

A number of quotes from news reports have been converted to paraphrases. It is my perception that rules for pulling quotes in the on-line blogging world are a bit looser than for books. Thus, there are no direct quotes in what you read here unless I have permission.

The series of posts certainly needs review by an experienced copyeditor. That oversight will not be applied so you can see the story as it unfolded in the way I described it at the time.

If you think you are a reasonably good writer in your correspondence, articles, or letters of recommendation, let me suggest an experience to build humility: have a copyeditor go over your material. My self-perception is that I'm an okay writer. That perception crashes every time I hire a copyeditor. Why explain this? So you know that I know the book is rough in places. That is by design.

Errors - Are there errors in this book?

You bet there are.

There are quite a few places where I had incorrect or incomplete information. Much of that is due to telling the story as it unfolded. Additional tidbits increase knowledge of the story. Gaining access to the federal PACER system, which makes available lots of documents of court cases, increased my knowledge a lot.

Those comments based on incomplete information will be left as they first appeared in print to show how the story developed.

Some things still aren't known.

I'm confident there are mistakes that I can't see. Probably some exist because I haven't pondered the story deep enough.

Perhaps there are even mistakes that others can't see because only Mr. London, Mr. Shaw, senior level staff of KPMG, various regulators, or prosecutors could provide the correct information. It may or may not be obvious, but none of those individuals saw any posts before publication and none of them saw any of this book before it was published.

Links - When the book was published, all the links worked. Although the internet is forever, specific pages can go away quite easily. For the print edition of this book, the links will be listed at the end of the paragraph.

In addition, live links will be posted at the publisher's web site. You can find the live links here:

http://riverstonefinancepress.com/tragedy-links/

That would be the publisher name (Riverstone Finance Press) dot com, slash, tragedy, hyphen, links.

Sequencing - The posts are primarily listed in the order they were published.

A few of them are reorganized for simplicity. Some of them, such as the consequence discussions, have been pulled together in a separate chapter.

The chronological sequence of posts lets you experience the story as it unfolded. Only a few misunderstandings or unknown details are corrected.

The date each post was published is listed after the post's title. Watch as the story unfolds.

There are rough edges, errors, and the book may read clunky at times. It isn't as polished as it could be. That is by design.

If my time allows and if there is interest from the accounting community, I may reorganize this material, do more research, and tell a more structured story. I have a few ideas on how to expand this into a full-length book. That is for another day.

In the meantime....

Consequences

You already know the end of the story: Scott London and his golf buddy, Bryan Shaw, are residing in a federal penitentiary as this book is published. Before we get into the details of the story, let's look at the consequences Mr. London has earned.

Consequences – insider trading edition #1
4/12/13

Let's examine the consequences on the horizon for Mr. Scott London, former KPMG partner, as a result of his indictment for allegedly trading on insider information.

(It was an information, not an indictment. I'll leave this and other comments as they were originally published.)

For some time I've been writing on the tragedy of fraud with a focus on the consequences that befall the perpetrator. I'll continue that discussion by looking at the public reports for this situation.

Is possible jail the only bad thing on the horizon?

Not quite. There's a long list of bad things in view.

As you read this, keep in mind my comments include a mixture of reported facts and my guesses & assumptions. I'll try to label the discussion accordingly.

Let's explore the consequences, assuming the reality is the same as what has been reported. Here's the list I can think of:
- Jail time
- Criminal fines
- Legal fees for criminal case
- Civil fines
- Criminal tax enforcement
- Publicity
- Loss of employment
- Loss of reputation
- Loss of professional license
- Limited future employability
- Litigation from employer
- Legal fees for civil litigation
- Financial devastation

Jail time

The alleged insider trading has led to a criminal indictment on one count for conspiracy to commit securities fraud through insider trading. (http://goo.gl/t2KuM4)

Multiple sources have said the maximum jail time is five years in prison. Mr. London's attorney is quoted as saying he will plead guilty at a May 19 hearing. It is up in the air what the sentence will be, but the feds have been pushing hard to get serious jail time for insider trading. (http://goo.gl/sqAeis)

Looks to me like time in the federal pen is likely.

Criminal fines

There are serious fines on the table as part of the criminal charges.

I've not researched the federal code, so will go with the maximum penalties outlined by Walter Hamilton in the Los Angeles Times, *In KPMG insider trading case, crime and blunders alleged*, Conspiracy for securities fraud is good for a maximum penalty of five years in prison a $250,000 fine. Could be up to double the gain on the fraud. (http://goo.gl/DlCojG)

Just trying to do insider trading can cost you $250,000. With allegedly successful trades on the table alleged by the SEC to have gains in the range of $1.27 million, the criminal penalty could be something in the range of $2.5 million. That of course assumes a conviction and further proof the SEC's numbers are correct. The numbers in the indictment are a little lower, I think.

Legal fees for criminal case

Mr. London retained a high-powered attorney. I have no clue what fees are involved to get that kind of talent on board. But I know the rates are going to be extremely high.

I'd also make a very wild guess that attorney will have several of his staff working the case. I'd make another wild guess that everyone involved has been working a lot of hours every week since the FBI's first visit.

That will cost a fortune.

Civil fines

The SEC has filed civil enforcement charges. I don't have enough experience in the public securities world to know what enforcement looks like for future employment bans or the additional civil penalties mentioned or any other consequences the SEC is asking for in items II, IV, and V at the end of the enforcement filing. (http://goo.gl/QG2eh8)

We can just look at item III which asks for disgorging illegal trading profits, which the SEC claims is $1.27 million.

That means likely penalty from the SEC is at least $1.27 million. I have no idea if there is a multiplier of some sort. Anyone care to comment on that?

Reports in the criminal indictment that Mr. London admitted that he disclosed inside information during his interview with the SEC and FBI might make it a bit hard to defend against the SEC's claims, although granting use immunity enters the issue in ways that I don't understand.

Consequences – insider trading edition – #2
4/15/13

Is possible jail the only bad thing on the horizon for a CPA accused of insider trading? Not quite. There's a long list of bad things within view.

This post discusses the possible consequences of:
- Criminal tax enforcement
- Publicity

Criminal tax enforcement

Tracy Coenen opens up the discussion of income tax fraud in her post *Scott London's Other Crime*. (http://goo.gl/OxvkW5)

After pointing out that an accountant ought to be able to get a better deal than something under $100K for something around $1.2M of illegal profits, she moves on to the tax issue.

She is making a not-so-wild guess that Mr. London probably didn't include the $50K of cash, $12K watch, and $12K or $20K of concert tickets in his 1040. Even if the concert tickets were worth a fraction of that, the numbers are substantial.

That could be something in the range of $60K to $80K over the years 2010 through 2012.

It is my guess that Big 4 partners have seriously messy tax returns because, based on my rather limited knowledge of partnership tax law, they pick up a tiny fraction of every income and expense line item of the firm.

As a result, I'll guess partners don't prepare their own returns. That means he would have had to tell the KPMG tax department to add another $10K or $30K of "other" income to his return each year. That would generate far too many questions, for which there wouldn't be good answers.

I'll agree with Ms. Coenen that chances are high that he didn't get those payments included on his 1040.

Thus, there is a good chance he may have some future conversations with the Criminal Investigation Department with follow-up criminal enforcement action.

That discussion likely ends with back taxes, interest & penalties, along with the possibility of more jail time.

One commenter at Ms. Coenen's post pointed out the California Franchise Tax Board will likely be paying Mr. London a visit. They will want money. Don't know if they push hard for jail time.

Publicity

Mr. London was featured on the front page of the Wall Street Journal on April 10.

He made it again on April 12. Twice in one week

Exhibit A to the criminal indictment is the FBI's photo of him accepting an envelope which the FBI claims contained a $5,000 payment.

You've seen the picture. It is plastered all over the internet. It's the illustrating photo for much of the reporting in the last few days. That's all the 'evidence' most readers will need to conclude he's guilty as sin.

That photo was at the top center of the WSJ's front page on 4/12, only without the grayed-out face on his golf buddy that appeared in the copy at the end of the indictment.

He also had reporters following him around which resulted in a background article at the Wall Street Journal – *Question in KPMG Case: Why?* The article gives the name of his wife, when he graduated from college (1984), his alma mater, name of the city where they live, when they bought their house and how much they paid for it, and background on one child (boy, attends a named high school, plays on baseball team). (http://goo.gl/hLmBGm)

Oh, and that article appeared on page B1 of the WSJ on 4-13 – that's the front page of the second section. Not the place I want to spread around my bio information. Hmm. Does that mean he made the front page of the WSJ three times in one week?

Most high-profile business writers have already run major articles discussing him and his alleged actions.

Every business writer in the country will be talking about him for the next few weeks.

Oh. And since we're in the internet age, most of those articles will never, ever go away. Some may disappear, but not many.

His great-great-grandchildren will be able to read almost all of those articles when they are surfing the 'net 70 or 80 years from now.

Consequences – insider trading edition – #3
4/16/13

Is possible jail the only bad thing on the horizon for a CPA who allegedly committed insider trading? Not quite. There's a long list of bad things within view.

This post discusses the possible consequences of:
• loss of employment,
• loss of reputation,
• loss of professional licensing

Loss of employment

Mr. London's employment was terminated week before last.

Public reports indicate he was the regional partner in charge of audit practice. That is a very major position which obviously would have very high levels of compensation.

Audit PIC. For the region. Of a Big 4 firm.

That is a dream position that few CPAs could ever hope to achieve. The opportunities, experiences, authority, and compensation would be astounding.

I have no idea what the comp is for a regional audit PIC of what is probably the second most lucrative region in the country. I'll make a wild guess it's over 1 million a year. Maybe two. By the way, I'm pulling numbers out of the air.

Even making a low assumption of $1M, that's a huge amount of money for a CPA. He was getting paid in a couple of weeks what many people make a year.

If you scoff at that amount, keep in mind he is producing more economic value for his employer than his salary.

He was creating far more economic value in one or two weeks with his brain than most people create in a year.

That income is gone.

He could have worked for another 10 or 15 years. That means he's out somewhere between $10 and $30 million.

Gone.

Loss of reputation

His reputation is shot.

Even if the publicity dies off this afternoon and even if the tax investigation doesn't go into the criminal realm and even if the SEC enforcement efforts were to somehow collapse and even if his attorney could successfully make an argument for no jail time and even if his current net worth is so large that he can absorb the financial hit to maintain his lifestyle and even if he can somehow afford retirement, his reputation is destroyed.

Completely, totally, utterly destroyed.

As the 'why did he do it?' conversation gets going, there will be dozens of business writers pondering in public the psychological makeup of the disgraced CPA. There will be tens or hundreds of thousands of readers pondering those arm-chair assessments wondering "is it narcissism, hubris, greed, or arrogance. Hmm, I think it was…". His friends, former colleagues, and buddies from the golf course will all be wondering.

How would you like to have around one-tenth of the professionals in your field working through an amateur assessment of your mental health?

Loss of professional license

If any of what's been alleged is proven true, is there any doubt the California Board of Accountancy will start enforcement action down the road?

I'm quite confident they will get involved. Think it through with me - his attorney said publicly he will plead guilty, which (if correct) means a felony conviction (which won't be going up for appeal if there's a guilty plea) for insider trading on client information obtained during the course of providing audit services. Yeah, they'll get involved.

Just as a guess, I think the most likely outcome of that journey will be the loss of his license.

The board obviously takes their time in enforcement actions, because they must of necessity let the criminal and civil cases run. That is a very good thing, by the way.

On the other hand, with the speed of the indictment and his attorney saying he plans to plead guilty in just over four weeks from now, the civil and criminal cases could be cleared up remarkably quick. The CBA might be able to move fast on this.

Fast or slow, I think we can all see the outcome.

So he's lost a great job, has destroyed his reputation, and will likely lose his CPA license. And the list of consequences isn't complete.

Consequences – insider trading edition – #4
4/17/13

Is possible jail the only bad thing on the horizon for a CPA accused of insider trading? Not quite. There's a long list of bad things within view.

This post will cover one possible consequence: the possibility of being sued by KPMG.

This series of posts is examining the consequences on the horizon for Mr. Scott London, former KPMG partner, as a result of his indictment for allegedly trading on insider information

Previous posts have discussed:
• Jail time
• Criminal fines
• Legal fees for criminal case
• Civil fines
• Criminal tax enforcement
• Publicity
• Loss of employment
• Loss of reputation
• Loss of professional license

Litigation from employer

The chairman and CEO of KPMG sent out a statement last Thursday evening. Let's just say he is not amused.

You can see the comment in quite a few places. I first read it in Francine McKenna's article at Forbes – *KPMG Statement on Scott London Criminal and Civil Charges*. (http://goo.gl/tMGlvl)

There are two particular items to note. The first comment was strong, referring to the severe breach of duties by Mr. London of his obligations to KPMG and their clients.

Early public comments indicated there were two clients involved. The criminal indictment said there were five. Sitting in my little corner of the audit world that was a surprise.

The CEO's comments above indicate that may have been a surprise to KPMG leadership. Again, I have no idea what happened behind closed doors, but reading between the lines, that comment suggests that Mr. London may have not fully disclosed the extent of his activities to his employer. I'm basing my wild guess on the additional details having become known. An alternative could be the brazenness and intentionality which became known after reading the allegation in the indictment.

Well that's just a guess on my part. An additional comment indicates KPMG will be taking legal action against Mr. London soon.

What could that involve?

For the non-CPAs in my audience, let me walk through what that comment means to me.

Remember that KPMG withdrew three years of audit opinions for Herbalife and two years for Sketchers?

That means another audit firm will have to be brought in to re-audit Herbalife for three years and re-audit Sketchers for two years.

That will cost a ton of money. How much?

Michael Rapoport gives a hint in the WSJ, *Bad Week for KPMG Could've Been Worse*. He reports KPMG's fees were $11.2M for three years at Herbalife and $1.7M for the 2011 audit of Skechers. (http://goo.gl/HVH86H)

On one hand, it won't take three times as long to re-audit three years as it would to audit one year. So there should be some savings from being able to do three sets of compliance tests or three sets of substantive tests all at the same time. You could test three sets of a particular disclosure for not much more time that it would take to test one year.

A lot of tests will be easier to perform with two year's hindsight. Two years after the fact it's really easy to test allowances for losses, whether for inventory, receivables, returns, or warranties.

On the other hand, the risk is far higher than usual for multiple reasons. So that means it could take longer to re-audit three years than to perform the three years initially.

Let's pull a number out of thin air by making the huge assumption that it will take as much time to re-audit as it did to perform the audits the first time. Let's also assume the Sketchers audit in 2012 cost as much as 2011.

So, taking the numbers mentioned by Mr. Rapoport, that would suggest the re-audit fees could be something in the range of $14.6 million (11.2 + 1.7 + 1.7).

Those two companies won't want to eat those costs. Why are they out that money? Because KPMG as a firm is no longer independent. The companies will likely look to KPMG to pick up the tab.

Sitting at my tiny little desk in my tiny little corner of the audit world I'm guessing that KPMG can either write a check today to reimburse the companies for those fees or they can write a check after they get sued. With my little bity understanding of risk management, seems to me KPMG would be far better off to put a blank check in the mail this afternoon. Or just have the new firms send their bills directly to the KPMG CEO.

KPMG is not going to want to absorb that $15 million hit. Why are they going to have to write the check? Because of Mr. London's alleged actions.

They will be looking to him to cover the cost.

Thus, we get back to the CEO's comment.

KPMG will be bringing legal actions against London in the near future.

(By the way, keep in mind I'm an accountant, not an attorney, and I'm not giving any stock advice, and my comments here are based on what I know from reading a lot over the last few days, and I'm just a little ol' sole practitioner. Wouldn't be wise to read more into what I say than what I actually said.)

There is a very good chance the former partner will lose his equity in the firm and his retirement. There is a smaller chance he could write a really big check to his former employer.

Attitudes inside firm

An anonymous article at Going Concern from a KPMG insider gives some hint of the mood inside the firm. Check out *KPMG Insider: Partners Felt Betrayed by Scott London's Actions*. If you're still reading my overly long post, you will want to check out that article. (http://goo.gl/tTNv3b)

In my opinion, the feelings of betrayal amongst partners described by the author are a strong indication this is a radical departure from the firm culture. If what is alleged is true, Mr. London appears to be an extreme outlier.

One major thing described by the author is the internal communication. Look at this comment to see the very clear, unadorned reaction from the CEO. An email from him says the email

> "…was one of the simplest and most powerful items I've seen come across the email in response to a firm event. Our chairman [John Veihmeyer] sent a simple email, just a few paragraphs, not even on the normal firm letterhead with his picture. Attached to the email was a copy of the complaint. In simple terms, the email said, "Everyone read this complaint. Read what this guy did. Know that we don't stand for it and know that we won't tolerate it." No BS, no fluff and no leaving it up to us to read the complaint on Going Concern. I've had a chance to have some candid conversations with John Veihmeyer before and this email reflected those. Pundits can pick it apart but for me it was the kind of response I wanted from my firm."

He sent out a copy of the indictment and asked everyone to read it. That e-mail is quite consistent with the restrained we-will-be-pursuing-legal-action comment in the press release last week.

Not only has the firm thrown him under the bus, sounds like they are going to put the bus in reverse and drive over him again. Then back up further, get a running start, and run over him with the other tires.

I'm thinking a suit to recover $15M for damages would be more educational for all the partners, professional staff and support staff than a dozen hours of ethics training. The message? If anyone else ever does this again, or anything even vaguely similar, rest assured the firm will grind you into dust.

No class time necessary – it would only take 2 emails. One attaching the text of the suit and the other with the court order to pay up.

So the answer to the question is yes, there are a lot of bad consequences to insider trading.

Consequences – insider trading edition – #5
4/18/13

Is possible time in jail the only bad thing on the horizon for a CPA accused of insider trading? Not quite. There's a long list of bad things within view.

This post will discuss:
- Poster child for (fill in the blank)
- Stress on marriage
- Impact on family

Poster child for (fill in the blank for your favorite agenda)

Mr. London will be cited as ultimate proof of whatever bias or prejudice an observer has.

After all, what do you expect from:
- the Big 4
- a CPA
- anyone who got their degree from a public college
- somebody in the big offices that doesn't have a clue about trying to get by in a small market – I'll betcha' he never had to hustle week after week to get another 25k engagement before the end of the year or lose his bonus
- a firm that doesn't disclose the name of the lead audit partner
- someone who's been around too long
- someone who came up through the ranks too fast
- a smug, fat-cat, capitalist pig who's obviously at the top of the 1%-ers
- the same firm that gave us that tax disaster

- someone in the ivory tower that never gets his hands dirty, 'cuz you know a regional audit PIC doesn't have a clue what it's like down here in the trenches

I've already heard or read five of the above comments.

For the next few years his name will be proof for a person's favorite hobby-horse. I think that's called confirmation bias.

Stress on marriage

I know nothing of his marriage other than he is married. The publicity, indictment, possible/likely jail, and financial trauma will put severe pressure on his marriage.

This trauma would be a strain on the healthiest marriage.

I hope his marriage stands strong in the midst of this and that he draws tremendous strength from his beloved. I sincerely hope she is able to help him through this trying time. I really do hope that.

Can you imagine the pain of having to tell your spouse the real reason for the FBI making a 6:00 a.m. visit to your home?

Can you image having to tell her that you likely will go to jail?

I'll make this next comment really vague – Once upon a time I had the opportunity to be in the room during a meeting in which a person confessed the scope of embezzlement to the employer while said person's spouse was present in the room. That was a horrible time. The look on that spouse's face is a major reason I wrote the tragedy of fraud series. (http://goo.gl/14Kb6g)

(Watch for many more aspects of the impact on his wife throughout this book.)

Impact on family

Can you imagine telling your little girl that her hero is going to jail? Yes my princess, daddy did some bad things.

In this case, published reports indicate the couple has two children, one of whom is a boy and plays on the high school baseball team. I'm sure the two children have better technology with better access to the 'net than me.

They have been able to follow the news and read all about the disaster as it unfolds.

They can also read the same snotty, mean-spirited comments at the end of news reports that I've read.

Can you imagine the pain of the conversations in which Mr. London had to tell his teenage children that what they will soon read in the papers is true? And that yes, he probably will go to jail?

Can you imagine the pain the children will have from the nasty comments they will get at school?

Mr. London will always know that he alone is the direct cause of every bit of his children's pain. He is the cause of his wife's tears.

(Many more comments to follow about the impact on his family.)

Consequences – insider trading edition – #6
4/19/13

Is possible time in jail the only bad thing on the horizon for a CPA accused of insider trading? Not even close. There's a long list of bad things within view.

This post will discuss:
- Fodder for armchair psychoanalysis
- Limited future employability
- Legal fees for civil litigation
- Financial devastation

Fodder for armchair psychoanalysis

If it is proved that he did what he is accused of doing, the "why?" conversations will run for months, if not years.

The conversations in print have already started.

Can you imagine being the subject of thousands of conversations by peers in your profession wondering about your mental state?

Is it arrogance? Hubris?

Greed? Stupidity? (I've already seen those comments in anonymous postings.)

Does he have some mental illness?

Is he a pathological liar? (Already saw that comment as if it was a statement of fact.)

There will be lots of published articles expounded at length on his motivations and character defects behind the motivation.

CPAs thinking in terms of the fraud triangle will pick apart news reports looking for motivation, opportunity, and rationalization.

The nastiness will run for a long time. Doesn't matter whether any of the pure speculation is true, or helpful, or grounded in even one fact, or contain any shred of logic.

The pseudo-psychological examinations will be around. For years. In print. Available to everyone with an internet connection.

Limited future employability

With the horrible publicity, visible firing, possible SEC sanctions, and possible loss of his license, his opportunities for gainful employment between now and when he hits retirement age are extremely limited.

I have no idea what the court orders look like in the federal system. For research on other blog posts I've written, I have read a few of the court orders for criminal cases in San Bernardino County, California, where I live. They contain clauses that make a person with financial skills essentially unemployable.

One set of court orders I read required the individual to disclose to a potential employer his conviction and the circumstances behind it. The individual is not allowed to have custody of anyone else's cash and cannot be a signer on someone else's bank account. That just about rules out any employment using the skills that particular person has.

From what I've read in the past, the SEC enforcement action will have some rather strong terms attached to it which will further limit employment opportunities with any company that has any involvement with the securities market.

How much you suppose his future earnings are going to drop? Think it will only be 90% (i.e. a drop to maybe $100k a year)? Or will be more like 95% or 98%?

Legal fees for civil litigation

It will take some serious time from some highly skilled attorneys to handle the litigation promised by KPMG.

That talent? Expensive.

The bill? Big.

Financial devastation

I can't even make any wild guesses on the final tally for all of the consequences I've listed. I'm thinking it will be measured as a percentage of his lifetime earnings. Perhaps an amount equal to 25%, 50%, or maybe 100% of all the money he's ever earned.

It is sufficient to say the impact on the family finances will be devastating.

Even if the CPA or his golf buddy have enough assets to cover the cost, it will be a catastrophe. There are very few people who could absorb those costs and still be financially stable afterwards.

Consequences – insider trading edition – the conclusion #7
4/20/13

Jail is really, really bad. Are there any other consequences on the horizon for a CPA accused of insider trading?

Oh yeah. There's a really long list of really bad things in the really near future.

Why this series?

My hope, perhaps just a silly dream, is that focusing on the horrible consequences that fall on the head of people who do bad things will deter a few people from doing bad things.

It's too late for Mr. London, but not for others.

The Consequences, not an exhaustive list

Let's revisit the consequences, making the big assumption that the reality is the same as what has been alleged.

The list of consequences is long and the impact huge.

- Jail time
- Criminal fines
- Legal fees for criminal case

16

- Civil fines
- Criminal tax enforcement
- Publicity
- Loss of employment
- Loss of reputation
- Loss of professional license
- Litigation from employer
- Poster child for favorite cause
- Stress on marriage
- Impact on family
- Fodder for armchair psychoanalysis
- Limited future employability
- Legal fees for civil litigation
- Financial devastation

Full disclosure:

I worked for Peat, Marwick, Mitchell before the name change to KPMG. I had the utmost respect for all my colleagues while working in the Albuquerque office. Still have a lot of respect for the firm. I've had no involvement with PMM/KPMG since leaving the firm, other than working for a bank which had PMM as their auditor. I run a one-person firm that is infinitesimally small compared to KPMG, so they aren't much competition for me (ahhh, maybe I should turn that the other way around….nah). Filter my comments as you wish.

Bryan Shaw pleads guilty for conspiracy in KPMG insider trading fiasco because he's guilty. Oh, and a really small additional consequence for Mr. London – #8
5/20/13

Comment from the 5/20 post is split into two parts. Here's the consequence:

Admitted payments to Scott London include $60k in cash, an expensive watch (claimed to be worth $12k), jewelry for Mr. London's wife (no description of items or value), and concert tickets, along with "expensive" meals. I've not seen indication of the size of Mr. London's total haul.

In addition to all the other consequences facing Mr. London, picture the look on his wife's face when she realized that really lovely piece of jewelry her husband picked out so carefully for their anniversary was actually from Mr. Bryan. And will cost jail time. And will likely go the U.S. Treasury.

You know it won't be a pleasant dinner when the conversation starter is: "So tell me honey, which of the pieces of jewelry you have lovingly given me in the last two years did you actually buy?"

**An additional consequence of insider trading –
knowing your name is in every newspaper in the country –
Former KPMG partner enters guilty plea – #9**
7/1/13

As expected, former regional audit PIC Scott London entered a guilty plea on Monday to one count of securities fraud. Sentencing is set for October 21, 2013.

In the 90 minutes since I saw the first report, over 30 hits show up on an internet search. I'm sure there will be many dozens more in the next few hours.

Three initial articles I saw:

• *Los Angeles Times* – *Former KPMG partner Scott London pleads guilty to insider trading* (http://goo.gl/m8oesl)

• *Bloomberg* – *Ex-KPMG Auditor London Pleads Guilty to Insider Trading* (http://goo.gl/GTfWtR)

• *Wall Street Journal* – *Former KPMG Partner Pleads Guilty to Securities Fraud* (http://goo.gl/VhkWzj)

Another interview with admitted inside-trader from KPMG
7/11/13
Two more minor consequences

He was able to break the news to his wife and son directly. Even though that was a very bad conversation (umm, honey, can we chat a minute about why the FBI wanted to talk to me this morning?), consider how their daughter got the news.

She read about it while in Barcelona studying there for the semester.

From the guilty plea on July 1 until the expected sentencing on October 22, look at the huge uncertainty hanging over his head:

A year in prison or 20. A fine equal to much of his liquid assets or all the investments he can readily liquidate. A civil suit or not with the costs running from merely big (for legal fees to get ready, just in case) to humongous (potential exposure enough to maybe wipe out his entire net worth).

He also expects he will be a pariah in the accounting world.

Yeah, I think so.

Consequences – insider trading edition – #10
10/21/13

Here are a few more consequences awaiting in the near future for Mr. Scott London, former KPMG partner, as he awaits sentencing after his guilty plea to trading on insider information.

These are pulled from his court filing in September. Going Concern has posted a copy of the filing by Mr. Scott London taking exception to the pre-sentencing report from the United States Probation Office. You can find the filing here. (http://goo.gl/iBXn7F)

Here are some more consequences and more detail on some I've mentioned before:

- Jail time – The sentencing report suggests 36 months. Mr. London's attorney is suggesting something in the range of 18-24 months is more appropriate.
- Criminal fine – The pre-sentencing report suggests a $100K fine. Mr. London's attorney suggests $25K.
- Legal fees – Take a look at that filing linked above. There was some serious legal time that went into drafting that filing. Those hours are expensive.
- Loss of current annual income of $900,000. This would run from now, when Mr. London is aged 51 through his mandatory retirement at age 60.
- Loss of appreciation on pension; identified as $2M over next 10 years.

Here is one I would not have guessed at:

- Complete loss of work friends and colleagues – All of his friends and acquaintances at KPMG are banned from having any contact with Mr. London in any manner. This is by KPMG direction. Seems to me a wise move. The consequence of that ban is none of them can give him any leads for possible future employment. Nor can they encourage or comfort him in his situation.

I'll update the list as more consequences come to mind.

Minor updates on insider trading fiasco at KPMG including more consequences
2/25/14

Since we are all anticipating the expected sentencing on Thursday for Mr. Scott London, regional audit PIC, lately of KPMG, here are two tidbits I've noticed over the last few months but haven't mentioned previously. Cost of re-auditing Herbalife will drop into the category of earned consequences when KPMG gets around to suing Mr. London. In older news, Mr. London updated his LinkedIn profile.

10/7 – LinkedIn profile: Mr. London is exploring other opportunities now that his status is "retired." His LinkedIn background admits a few blemishes in his work experience (which I will quote verbatim since it is intended to be a public document and I think easily subject to fair use in a critical article):

> Well, a lot has changed over the last year. After making a mistake that cost me my career with a Big 4 accounting Firm and

19

> I am looking forward to starting over again. (sic for clumsy phrasing) While I have lost credibility (deservedly so), there is a lot that I have to offer future employers. …
>
> Yes, I regret my past actions this year, but I am looking forward to a future in which I can assist another company as they address the challenges in business today.

As of 2/24 those comments are still on the profile except for the sentence about losing credibility. That's been deleted. Not that there is any near-term need for finding another employer, but that is a bit much.

Only item listed in experience is Partner at KPMG US from July 1995 through March 2013. Attended Cal State Northridge, graduating in 1984. Job title is 'Financial Consultant.'

He has 357 connections, which probably aren't particularly useful now, since everyone at KPMG is prohibited from having any contact with him. Connections at former clients probably won't be replying to any messages.

Cost of reauditing Herbalife

12/16 – Wall Street Journal – Herbalife says "No Material Changes" Found in Reaudit - Last paragraph says PwC charged about $15 million to reaudit three years of financials. (http://goo.gl/Mpc37a)

My guess? Herbalife sends a copy of the bill to KPMG who then writes a check in return for an unconditional release. Or maybe they just send a check to avoid a few extra days of legal fees. KPMG then sits on the bill until all other proceedings against Mr. London are done and then sues him to recover the $15M.

Now we can quantify that part of the well-earned consequences from Mr. London's insider trading.

More consequences of insider trading – #11
2/27/14

Previous post explained Mr. Scott London surrendered his CPA license as a consequence of his guilty plea to insider trading. This discussion will go through the timing of the disciplinary process and outline a few more well-deserved consequences Mr. London has earned. (http://goo.gl/AqAO3d)

Update #74, which contains a summary of the action, can be found here. (http://goo.gl/6GPQw5)

Timing

The disciplinary order has the Accusation attached to it. Here's the timing, which is interesting because I've never looked at one of these in detail.

The federal PACER system shows a plea agreement was entered on 7/1/13.

Complaint AC-2014-10 is dated 8/21/13. It contained three causes for discipline, all of which are rolled into the comments published in Update #74.

The stipulation agreement says that Mr. London admits all the accusations. In the harsh legal words used in such admissions:

> "Respondent admits the truth of each and every charge and allegation in Accusation No. AC-2014-10, agrees that cause exists for discipline and hereby surrenders his Certified Public Accountant License No. 46174 for the CBA's formal acceptance."

Mr. London signed the stipulation on 10/15/13.

An Assistant AG for the state signed it on 10/28/13.

The disciplinary action was dated 11/27/13 and became effective 12/27/13.

Other consequences

Small dollar penalty –

If Mr. London were to apply for reinstatement of his license, he will have to reimburse CBA $1,637.50 for costs of the investigation. Since that is a conditional payment and I think it is unlikely he will reapply, that isn't really a consequence. For one thing, if he reapplies, the settlement specifically says everything in it will be considered as a part of his request.

Legal costs –

Mr. London retained legal counsel to represent him in the disciplinary process. Usually malpractice insurance would cover the legal costs of a state investigation. I'm guessing that Big 4 partners don't carry malpractice insurance as individuals. I think that means he paid this attorney out of his own pocket. It is separate counsel from the attorney who handled the federal criminal case. So you can count the legal costs for this action as another part of the earned consequences of his illegal behavior.

Quick action –

This action by CBA moved fast. The complaint was filed (8/21) about seven weeks after his plea deal (7/1). The negotiations for settlement were resolved in another eight weeks (10/15). The deal was official after about six weeks (11/27) and was effective a month later (12/27).

This moved fast. I would have guessed this might take a year or more for the disciplinary action to be finished. My guess on why it moved so quickly is that Mr. London readily agreed to surrender his license.

Self-identification in your job -

Here's another consequence, this time in the emotional realm.

Many people get their identity from their work. This is even more so for men – we guys often get our sense of worth from our work. That's why lots of guys have a real struggle when they retire. I'm guessing this is even more pronounced for those of us in professional fields.

21

Last fall, Mr. London signed away his professional credentials. He's been an accountant since college and was a well-respected and well-compensated Big 4 partner for 18 years.

It's a wild guess, but I'll make a guess that he has a large part of his identity and self-worth tied up in being a CPA.

He signed that away on 10/15 and saw his license officially disappear on 12/27. That has likely caused a hurt that will take a long time to heal.

Please keep in mind I'm not complaining about his consequences or feeling sorry for him. He worked hard to earn every little bit of the consequences he is getting.

Why this discussion then?

This specific situation provides a great study for the rest of us about the consequences of our actions. I hope this will be a learning opportunity for all of us.

Full disclosure: Just so everyone knows, the California Board of Accountancy is the regulatory agency with oversight authority of my CPA practice. Also, I worked for KPMG for a few years, way back when it was call Peat, Marwick, Mitchell.

Judicial consequences and small consequences
for insider trading – #12
4/24/14

Now we can count some of the hard and soft consequences in Scott London's insider trading journey.

Jail time

From news reports of the day, here is his sentence:
- 14 months in jail
- 36 months probation after jail
- Unknown community service after jail
- $100,000 fine.

He must report by July 18. One minor consequence is he knows for the next 85 days he will have to walk into jail. I would make a wild guess the anticipation of that will produce quite a few sleepless nights.

I'll have more detail when the official sentencing document is available on-line.

Just like the TV show Cheers,
eeeeverybody knows your name

Here is a small consequence:

He gets to see his name splashed all across the twitterverse and tons of news reports.

At 6:30 the evening of his sentencing, I did a fast browse on Twitter for "Scott London." A cursory review found 12 different people tweeting with that exact phrasing, plus my tweets. Those 12 people have about 72,000 followers. Didn't check for any other wording. (Didn't include my

0.05K followers.) Granted there's a lot of overlap of followers in that group, but still…a huge number of people saw tweets about his sentencing.

In addition, a search on Google for "Scott London" identified 64 news articles in the last six hours on his sentencing. My two posts weren't picked up in the search yet.

I'll make a guess the front page of the Wall Street tomorrow covers the sentencing. What do you think the odds are on that famous photo being on the front page? Again.

The sentencing will be in the next issue of every business magazine and in many newspapers tomorrow.

Update: Wow, I called that one wrong. The Wall Street article was on page C3. No photo at all.

Additional consequences of insider trading – #13
6/29/14

On June 25, 2014, Scott London was interviewed at length in a webcast presented by The Pros and The Cons. During the interview, Mr. London shared several more aspects of the consequences of his illegal insider trading. (http://goo.gl/ZOJqVO or www.theprosandthecons.com)

Add the following items to the long list of consequences of illegal behavior.

Knowing you will be a case study decades into the future – after one interviewer mentioned this would be a great case study for the Harvard Business Review, Mr. London said he knows that will be the case. He hates to be the subject of case studies but doesn't think there would be a better example.

Embarrassment for your child during a college class – Mr. London's older child, a daughter, is studying accounting. One day in class they were discussing ethics with Mr. London's situation as the topic of the day. Great.

Mr. London's daughter gets to sit in class as they discuss the foolishness of her dad. Imagine having your daughter sitting through a discussion of how stupid and foolish her dad is and wondering how long he's been doing this illegal stuff and some of the students sure do hope he gets a lot of jail time.

Just imagine the number of times his daughter will hear the comment over the next 20 years: "Nice to meet you. You said London.. London… Are related to that guy from KPMG?"

Embarrassment for your extended family – Mr. London's brother was recently playing racquetball with a buddy. The buddy was joking around, wondering on the court how his brother will look in zebra stripes.

Those close to you get to tell you how stupid you were – Shortly after the visit from the FBI, Mr. London explained the whole situation to his wife, who had no clue what was going on. At the end of the explanation her comment was "that's the most stupid thing you've ever done."

When he explains things to close friends the usual comment is to say something like "that was stupid."

Comment from one person was "What the h*** were you thinking?"

Extended financial consequences – Mr. London indicated that with a felony conviction he will not be able to refinance his house. I wasn't aware of that, and hadn't thought about it, but it makes sense. A felony conviction would be a pretty severe risk factor for anyone who's looking at a credit decision.

There's no place to park your investments – He indicated he was asked (I doubt it was much of a request) to close his investment accounts. So where would you move your investments? How could you ever hold mutual funds, stocks, or bonds again if no one will let you open an account?

Harm to charities you believe in – You serve on a charity's board of directors because you believe in their cause and want to help them. Mr. London was asked to resign all of his board memberships. Each of those charities has also suffered direct consequences. He did not go into details, but the publicity of his illegal behavior hurt the charities he believed in.

The consequences of criminal behavior just keep piling up.

Public comments on compensation for inside trading CPA partner
8/22/14

There are a range of comments in public about the comp package for former KPMG partner Scott London, who is now in federal prison for insider trading. How can we reconcile those amounts?

High estimate

Francine McKenna speculated in one of her articles that her sources suggested Mr. London was earning a salary of between $1.5M and $2M. I mentioned this comment on April 21, 2013.

Mid-range estimate

The defense team's Objection to PSR (presentencing report) was filed with the court on September 23, 2013. I have a copy of the filing. The document is inside the federal PACER system and I don't know how to link to it so you can see it. Thus, you can't read the comment for yourself. Discussed it previously in my post on October 21.

(Update: Going Concern has the document available here.)

(http://goo.gl/idn1RM)

Page 10 has a list of the various impacts on Mr. London's future earnings capacity from the criminal charge. This is in the context of an argument against the $100,000 fine. In the filing, Mr. Braun (defense counsel) says:

"Mr. London's loss of income is summarized as follows:

"Loss of annual income of $900,000 for the next 10 years. (Scott has just turned 51 and the mandated retirement age at KPMG is 60.)"

(Update: By the way, I'm quoting without permission because materials in PACER are public documents.)

Low estimate

Quentin Fottrell interviewed Scott London. His report is *Confessions of an insider trader on the eve of his prison sentence*. I discussed this on June 21. (http://goo.gl/zV4zNW)

In the interview, Mr. London indicated his salary was more like $650K.

How to put those numbers together?

So, we have three estimates:

- $1.5M or more, maybe $2M
- $900K
- $650K.

First guess

My best wild guess on reconciling those numbers is that the high number is possibly the profit allocation to his account, with a huge portion required to be retained in the capital account. Maybe the $900K is the amount allowed to draw with the $650K possibly being the actual draw net of withholding to cover estimated payments. Or perhaps the $650K is the draw allowed this year against the balance in the capital account last year.

Second guess

Or is the reference to a $650K amount just public modesty? Unless you are in the entertainment world, pro sports, or at the peak of the business world, our society doesn't like talking directly about the amount of dollars in the paycheck.

Do you suppose the $900K and $650K are modesty?

Third guess

I'm guessing the compensation formulas for partners in large firms are complex. Probably a combination of base salary, return on capital account, extra for large book of business or high-profile clients, and huge bonuses for making lots of rain. Think back to partnership accounting in your advanced class to recall that after the various formulas are applied, the balance left over still needs to be allocated. So the amount going into the capital account finally includes an allocation of the extra or shortfall after all the above allocations are made.

If that wild guess is vaguely on track, then perhaps the three cited amounts (1.5m, 900k, 650k) are some combination of the various factors that go into the comp structure.

2 comments on the post:

I would be cautious before presuming that the figures you cite are in conflict. There are many ways that these amounts could be both consistent and reasonably accurate.

For example, the $650K might be Mr. London's base salary, while the higher amounts could include bonuses, profit sharing, and/or deferred compensation. To the best of my knowledge, large CPA partnerships distribute profits at least annually, because partners don't want their at-risk capital accounts to become bloated, so it is unlikely that 100% of Mr. London's compensation was salary-based. Also, Ms. McKenna is unlikely to report a subtotal without identifying it as such.

The difference between $900K and $1.5M could also be caused by the inclusion or exclusion of bonuses, profit sharing and/or deferred compensation. If there is variable deferred compensation, opposing experts might calculate the value using different valuation assumptions or estimates (for example, "normalization adjustments" to amounts considered non-recurring or anomalous). Or one figure might be from last year, while the other two figures are three and five year averages.

Keith Mautner - FAILSAFE-CPA.com

(http://www.failsafe-cpa.com/)

Keith:

Most important part for nonaccountants to realize is your idea that all the amounts may be correct with the appropriate label. Partner compensation is based on multiple complex components. That also means comp can go up and down easily. As you mentioned, the amounts could be actual last year, estimate of this year, average of recent years, or expectation for next decade.

Thanks for taking time to comment.

Jim

Please remember that links to articles on the internet have a short URL at the end of the paragraph linking to the article. For example:

(http://goo.gl/yjh2rb)

In addition, live links are available at the publisher's web site. You can find the live links at:

http://riverstonefinancepress.com/tragedy-links/

The story explodes

Live example of the 'Wall Street Journal' test
4/10/13

If you want to test a decision, ask yourself how this will look on the front page of the Wall Street Journal. (http://goo.gl/yjh2rb)

We see an example of that test in today's WSJ.

Front page.

Above the fold.

Big font covering 4 columns.

Here's the headline:

Trading Case Embroils KPMG
Partner who Audited Herbalife and Skechers Admits Giving Stock Tips to Friend
(http://goo.gl/iYeUNm)

How's that looking?

The partner, from the LA office, gets to see how his actions look.

On the front page.

Of the Wall Street Journal.

What did he do?

Allegedly chat about clients in the context of a buddy wondering what stocks to buy. And getting stuff, including a few wads of cash, in return. The FBI allegedly recorded him taking one envelope containing $5,000. In currency.

That's called insider trading.

Thus far the accusations have cost him his job, his reputation, the legal fees of hiring a high-powered attorney, and an interview with the FBI & SEC. Before he's got this wrapped up (assuming he actually did anything that is reported), it could possibly cost him everything in his retirement accounts, all his equity at KPMG, all his investments, and his CPA license. With the push from the SEC on insider trading, probability of time in the federal pen is greater than remote.

That does not look good on the front page of the WSJ.

Update: You can modify this to the "LA Times test" if you live in Southern California.

Illustration of the concept: The Los Angeles Times article, *Fired KPMG auditor can't explain 'lapse of judgment'* starts the article with the partner's name. They have 15 major articles posted on-line about this story as of Wednesday evening. (http://goo.gl/fxMHR6)

That doesn't look good either.

Update: Second failure of the test shows up a few days later, with a color picture.

Initial highlights of insider trading by KPMG partner
4/10/13

A now-former partner of the LA office of KPMG, Scott London, is in boiling hot water for alleged insider trading.

Lots of news out. I will give a general overview. Lots more news will be out in the next few days, I'm sure.

Brief outline

He allegedly gave ideas about companies where he was the audit partner to a buddy at a golf club. The feds tumbled to odd trading patterns in said buddy's portfolio and investigated.

The former partner hired an attorney before his first interview with the FBI and SEC. That's a good move.

For more background, check out _Golf Pal Chats Led to Probe_ – _Wall Street Journal._ (http://goo.gl/EWVvaM)

The basic details are the partner has been fired. According to _Trading Case Embroils KPMG_ at the WSJ, in return for the info he provided, a discounted watch, some dinners out and from $1,000 to $2,000 on a few occasions. Exact word was a couple, which usually means two. (http://goo.gl/fZ3uyW)

Pulling opinions on 2 audits

KPMG has resigned from two audits. They've also pulled opinions on Herbalife for three years and Skechers for two year. KPMG reportedly said they weren't aware of errors in the financial statements.

I'm scratching my head about that. Pulling 3 years of opinions on one client and 2 years on the other. I think there's more to come on this story.

No coverage of legal fees

Francine McKenna had one of the first articles I saw Wednesday morning – _Another 'Rogue' Audit Partner'; Another 'Duped' Audit Firm._ (http://goo.gl/cgNqXI)

She provides a survey of Big 4 partner's flops on insider trading.

She also reports KPMG won't be paying the partner's legal fees. He's on his own.

More background

The partner is identified in the Los Angeles Times article, _Fired KPMG auditor can't explain 'lapse of judgment'_ as a 29-year veteran of the firm. He is the audit PIC for the Pacific Southwest region of KPMG. (http://goo.gl/MYAjFc)

A regional PIC?

The article says he has 900 staff working for him.

Rough timeline

Two *LA Times* articles you want to read:

- *Visit from FBI the end for auditor in KPMG insider-trading scandal* (http://goo.gl/4nbsGN)
- *KPMG auditor was photographed accepting cash bribe over coffee* (http://goo.gl/zPzmp4)

The partner's golf buddy, who has now been identified, tells us when the info was flowing from 2010 until 2012. He says he got non-public information and traded on it.

He has been working with the FBI, SEC and Department of Justice for several months:

A few weeks ago, the buddy gave the partner an envelope with $5,000 in it while they had coffee at a Starbucks. The FBI recorded the payment.

A few days later the FBI showed up at the partner's home and showed him the pictures. They advised him to get an attorney. That was a couple of weeks ago.

Tip for everyone reading this post – if anyone ever, ever hands you an envelope with tons of money in it, get up and walk away.

Last week the FBI notified KPMG the partner was under investigation. He was fired within 24 hours.

KPMG partner indicted for insider trading. Indictment shows fiasco is far worse than shown in initial reports
4/11/13

The KPMG insider trading fiasco is far worse that indicated in first reports.

- The amounts allegedly paid to the partner are larger than initial reports.
- The government alleges confidential information was passed on 5 companies, not 2.
- The government alleges the CPA partner actively planned with his golf buddy when to buy and sell which stocks and options.

The Wall Street Journal had the first report I saw announcing Scott London, regional PIC at KPMG in LA has been indicted for securities fraud on Thursday morning – Substantially expanded article from the first announcement is here: *Former KPMG Partner Charged*.

(http://goo.gl/1szju4)

The indictment is available on Fox Business – *Ex-KPMG Exec Charged in Insider Trading Scam*. (http://goo.gl/OiEmiH)

The indictment has a number of interesting comments:

- There are wiretaps involved as evidence
- Allegation is the golf buddy made $1M in profits off the inside information

- The partner allegedly provided info about earnings announcements and guided the golf buddy how to structure the trades to avoid detection.
- There are allegedly three more KPMG clients involved – Deckers Outdoor Corporation, RSC Holdings, and Pacific Capital Bancorp (pages 3 to 9).
- The golf buddy alleges he gave money to the CPA roughly equal to 10% of his gains. He claims to have handed off $10K bundles of $100 bills (page 10)
- The golf buddy alleges he spent between $25k to $40K for concert tickets for himself and the CPA. He also alleges he gave a $12K watch to the partner.
- The golf buddy alleges the partner volunteered that Herbalife would be a good stock to buy.
- The FBI alleges that during the meeting when the golf buddy passed $5k to the CPA, they discussed how to make money in Herbalife stock.
- The FBI claims to have recorded conversations on 2-21-13 between the two discussing how the Deckers stock price will react to the as-yet-nonpublic earnings release that was about to go out.
- The FBI claims to have audio and visual of a meeting on 3-7-13 in the parking lot of a coffee shop. The FBI alleges $5k was passed and the two discussed whether to cashing out some Decker's options.
- On 3-20-13 the FBI told the CPA he was under investigation (page 22)
- On 4-3-13 the FBI interviewed the CPA at the US Attorney's Office. The CPA was provided an agreement for use immunity of the interview. (page 22)
- The FBI claims the CPA admitted to sharing information on 4 clients and wasn't sure about a 5th. (page 23)
- The FBI claims the CPA estimates he received about $50k in cash for the information. (page 23)

The indictment is also available in the WSJ article at this link. (http://goo.gl/q4vbLO) (http://goo.gl/0cvKoI)

Full disclosure: I worked at Peat, Marwick, Mitchell, as KPMG was known back then, for about 3 years in their Albuquerque office. I have high respect for my colleagues at PMM and the firm of KPMG.

SEC files complaint against former KPMG partner
4/11/13

The SEC has filed a civil action against former KPMG partner Scott London and his golf buddy accusing them of trading on inside information.

You can read the SEC's press release here and see a copy of the complaint here.

You can read the WSJ's article here and find the SEC's complaint here. (http://goo.gl/q4vbLO) (http://goo.gl/FMTMML)

The SEC alleges that the golf buddy made illegal profits of at least $1.27M (paragraph 7 on page 2).

Whether the SEC's or FBI's estimate of gains is correct, my recollection of several on-line articles suggests those amounts indicate the pair is exposed to some serious jail time.

KPMG partner arraigned – might plead guilty – hint on how to avoid jail time?
4/11/13

Former KPMG partner Scott London was arraigned today according to several news reports. He is free on $150,000 bail.

His attorney suggested Mr. London will plead guilty at the May 17 hearing.

Check out:
- Wall Street Journal – *Secret Recordings, Cash in Insider Sting* - info on court hearing is in the 7th paragraph (http://goo.gl/gJyKBI)
- Los Angeles Times – *Former KPMG auditor Scott London appears in court* – good picture of Mr. London and his attorney. (http://goo.gl/jwNdIq)
- Bloomberg – *Ex-KPMG Partner London Will Plead Guilty, Lawyer Says* - best of the three articles (http://goo.gl/p3z8vv)

An idea on why there's the admission during first interview and likely fast guilty plea

Struck me as odd that he admitted to sharing inside information for profit in his first interview with the FBI, SEC and USAG. I've seen the same comment elsewhere. Walter Pavlo discussed that at Forbes this morning, before the indictment appeared: *Former KPMG Partner Scott London's Legal Strategy: Admit Guilt Before Charges*. (http://goo.gl/fzM5mX)

Also seems odd to me as a businessman that immediately after arraignment his attorney said he plans to plead guilty. Seems it would be sort of hard to cut a deal after that.

In the Bloomberg article by Edvard Pettersson, Mr. London's attorney, Harland Braun, said he thinks his client will plead guilty on May 17, the next hearing.

No argument. No plea deal. Already saying in public his client will plead guilty.

Jail time? His attorney expects none

How could that be? The Feds have been making a major push for years to get hard time for insider trading.

Does this comment give you a hint as to the argument that might be made at sentencing for no jail time?

His attorney says Mr. London was honest when confronted, which avoided a major investigation at KPMG. Possibly hundreds of clients could have been involved. It might even have caused a stock crash, according to Mr. Braun. The attorney said Mr. London had not idea that Mr. Shaw made as much money as he did.

Hmm. Maybe the fast admission, full cooperation, and no-fuss guilty plea will be combined with the argument that by doing so, the ex-partner prevented the catastrophic damage of investigating hundreds of audits and a shock to the entire stock market.

In return for avoiding a systemic shock, maybe he should be able to walk.

Does that look like a possibility to anyone else? Am I reaching?

Failing the front-page-of-
The-Wall-Street-Journal test twice in one week
4/12/13

"How will this look on the front page of the Wall Street Journal?" is a handy question to use when pondering what to do about an accounting or auditing issue. It's useful for any business decision.

I've used that for myself and as an illustration for clients and other people I'm talking to. It provides a good way to frame up how a decision will look to other people.

For the second time this week, Mr. Scott London, formerly a partner at KPMG, has seen how this question plays out.

The front page of the Wall Street Journal today has a headline across three columns:

Secret Recordings,
Cash in Insider Sting
(http://goo.gl/UXsFKL)

How would you like to be the subject of the article?

Above the title is a color photo, about 3" by 4" provided by the FBI. It first appears to the world as Attachment A to the indictment.

In the unlikely event you haven't actually seen the picture yet, the FBI asserts it is of Mr. London receiving an envelope containing $5,000, which is an alleged payment from his golf buddy to him sharing the proceeds of insider trading.

Check out the second paragraph to see the ex-partner's name.

Check out the third paragraph which gives more details of the depth of the alleged insider trading and that the FBI claims it has recordings. Mr. London passed on notice about earnings releases and merger plans. Calls between the two were recorded in 2013 and Mr. Shaw was wired during their recent meetings.

Read between the lines on the fourth paragraph which relays the information Mr. London provided earlier in the week. He previously said the parcels contain one or two thousand and that only happened a couple of times. He also said that his comments were only general assessments of whether a specific company was doing well or not.

You can reach your own conclusions on Mr. London telling the WSJ reporters one thing and dramatically more serious information showing up in the indictment a day later.

Unlike telling untruths to the feds, which is a felony, telling stories to a newspaper reporter isn't going to get you jail time. You just look really, really bad when you read about two different stories on the front page of the WSJ.

And all that stuff is on the front page. Of the Wall Street. Above the fold. With a color photo.

This is the meaning of the old 'front page of the newspaper test.'

Here's my post from earlier this week: _Live example of the 'Wall Street Journal' test_.

Background articles emerging on KPMG insider trading fiasco
4/13/13

A few articles of interest out today on the alleged insider trading by former KPMG partner Scott London.

Wall Street Journal – _Question in KPMG Case: Why?_

(http://goo.gl/rnWaLT)

Some general background in the article. Previous public reporting has indicated Mr. London is married with two children.

This article reports that during this week one of their sons was playing in a high school baseball game attended by Mr. London and his wife. He graduated from college in 1984. My inference is he started with Peat Marwick, since that would give him the reported 29 years tenure at KPMG.

Mr. London is the son of a CPA.

(Update - at age of 52, Mr. London is young enough that there's a good chance his father is still alive. Imagine his dad having to read about his son getting arrested. Imagine having to explain this to your CPA dad.)

The two children include one son in high school. Just as a wild guess, the other child is somewhere in that age range. That will be mentioned later in one of my posts on consequences.

The family bought a house in Agoura Hills in 1995 for $434K. Since they are still living in that community and there is no other mention of another house, I assume they are still living in the house they bought in

1995. That was 11 years after graduation, which would be about the time he was promoted to partner.

His income has blossomed since 18 years ago, yet they live in the same home. That's the modest lifestyle you would expect from a CPA. That reinforces the tremendous questions of why?

Wall Street Journal – *How to Solve a Problem Like Scott London*. (http://goo.gl/Hx5XZP)

How can a CPA firm absolutely, positively prevent this type of disaster?

Article explores the question.

I have no clue what kind of training and requirements the Big 4 have in place for independence issues, so the following comments are quite useful for me.

All the firms have training programs emphasizing the need for confidentiality. They have whistleblower programs. Staff have to attest annually they are in compliance.

I've no doubt there is very clear training that says quite explicitly that most of what you see while working at whichever firm is confidential and must be guarded. Whistleblower systems put staff on notice someone could turn you in if you are doing stupid stuff visibly.

Is there any doubt that any accountant that's worked for any of the firms more than six months or anyone who's even gotten to the point of studying for the exam knows confidential stuff can't be shared? I don't think so.

Some firms require senior staff to provide details of their personal investments.

That's good. But it won't detect giving tips to your buddy, your wife, or lover. It won't detect an undisclosed account at another broker.

His attorney said Mr. London signed all the required compliance documents. He knew the information passed to his buddy was confidential

Good. But again, the absolute knowledge that what you are doing is wrong doesn't stop a person if said person wants to do something wrong.

So, after all that stuff, the question still stands. How do you absolutely prevent insider trading?

Los Angeles Times – *Timeline of alleged insider-trading dealings involving London*. (http://goo.gl/wZDdQ9)

Article summarizes the known stock activity and gains into a timeline by company as alleged by the FBI.

KPMG insider trading update – 4-15-13 –
fibbing about college baseball?
4/15/13

As most CPAs scramble to take care of the last few details tonight, I'll give a quick summary of the news about Mr. Scott London, the now-former partner from KPMG who allegedly was engaged in some insider trading.

Not much news over the last few days after a frantic week. I haven't seen anyone come up with a vaguely plausible answer to "why?"

Here's a bit of update:

Francine McKenna has a recap of the last week in her post, _Early Returns: Scott London, KPMG and Another Partner Trading on Inside Information_. The article provides background on three other insider trading messes created by Big 4 partners. (http://goo.gl/Pc9tbL)

She also gives me a shout out for my coverage and links to two posts. Thanks!

Wall Street Journal reporter Jean Eaglesham says the Scott London case illustrates that the _Limits of Insider Probes Expand_. Bringing surveillance, video recording, and wiretaps to the table for a so-called small insider trading case shows the seriousness such cheating is gathering from the feds. (http://goo.gl/UqCNLQ)

The article points out that the SEC has filed 26 insider trading cases since October. The total count of firms and staff accused since fall of 2009 is over 430.

The techniques otherwise seen in organized crime cases combined with the level of detail in the indictment and adding a photo as an exhibit seem to point toward sending a message. Seems like the feds want everyone to know they are serious – don't do insider trading.

Fibbing about college baseball experience

The Huffington Post reports _Scott London, KPMG Partner Accused of Insider Trading, Lied About Baseball Career_. (http://goo.gl/cheguq)

Key paragraph says Mr. London claimed to be on the baseball team in college. That claim was made in a press release from the Los Angeles Sports Council when they announced Mr. London had been elected chairman of that NPO in 2011.

Only problem is that the college went through their old media documents and couldn't find him listed as a player anywhere.

The article points out that info first surfaced in an article in the Los Angeles Times, _Ex-KPMG partner was sting target_. Check out the third to last paragraph. (http://goo.gl/UAjH5h)

I really don't understand that part of the story. It is just so easy to check things like what sports you played in college. Why make that up? It doesn't add anything and isn't necessary.

(Hat tip: _Going Concern._)

Ponderings

I'll circle back later to discuss the posts that ponder the implications. For the moment you can check out:

Re:Balance – *KPMG's Independence, Herbalife's Stock Price, and the Game of Name Blame.* Jim Peterson discusses the lack of any impact on stock prices from the auditor of one of the clients losing independence and the likely impact of the fiasco on the push to disclose partner's names, an issue which he asserts has no impact on the broken audit model. (http://goo.gl/9yXx4L)

Grumpy Old Accountants – *Insider Trading or Lack of Transparency: Which is the Bigger Sin?* Professor Anthony Catanach ponders the independence issue and what could be so wrong as to lead someone into this mess. (http://goo.gl/PMovQe)

Far, far too much in each column to even start giving justice in one sentence. Guess you need to check them out yourself. I'll come back to those later.

KPMG insider trading update
4/21/13

Not much news the last few days. Only two articles I wanted to highlight that discuss the allegations of insider trading against former KPMG partner Scott London:

Francine McKenna University of Chicago's Capital Ideas blog – *What's wrong with insider trading?* (http://goo.gl/YW1FBn)

Post starts by providing a recap of other Big 4 insider trading cases.

She then provides some guesses on what compensation levels may be in play. After visiting with her sources, she estimates a partner with the level of responsibility for supervising 50 audit partners would be drawing a salary between $1.5 million and $2 million a year.

Ms. McKenna raises a couple of questions for future discussion – should insider trading even be illegal and should there be prohibitions on auditors having financial interest in clients.

***Update*:** *I don't know where those ideas are going. She and some other writers are a long way ahead of me on those concepts. I suppose with the technology we have today, we could drop the ban on insider trading in return for instantaneous disclosure of insider trades and maybe monthly disclosures of positions from all insiders.*

One of the last comments highlights that the stock market didn't have much reaction to the breaking news that KPMG hadn't been independent for three years. I've seen two interpretations of that info. Will take some time to sort out what that means.

Michael Rapoport, *Wall Street Journal, KPMG Plans Review Amid Trading Case.* (http://goo.gl/4fl1NR)

As you would expect, KPMG will review their rules to see if there is room for improvement. The article provides background on their policies:

KPMG's code of conduct, which all KPMG employees must agree to comply with each year, says insider trading is "prohibited." It adds that employees "should not disclose any confidential or private information to third parties" and should share it with other KPMG employees only on "a need-to-know basis."

The code also warns employees against a variety of practices that could lead to leaks of confidential information, like discussing the information in public, using unencrypted "thumb drives" for client data, and leaving documents or data in unsecured places like unlocked cars and restaurant coat checks. Documents with confidential information are supposed to be placed in secure bins for shredding when they are disposed of.

Based on just a four sentence summary (which is all I know about their policies) that sounds good. Should make it quite obvious to anyone who can read that it would be very wrong to do the things alleged by the Department of Justice.

One tidbit of interest is the estimated amount of audit fees for the region for which Mr. London had PIC responsibilities. Mr. Rapoport estimates the audit fees of the region's clients are around $105 million a year, based on his review of regulatory filings from those clients.

KPMG insider trading update – 4-22-13
4/22/13

A few articles of interest today on the alleged insider trading mess at KPMG.

I'll start by giving yet one more illustration to the ol' question:

Q: Why should we be very careful with Facebook comments?

A: You may read them again.

In the *Los Angeles Times*.

And at *Going Concern*.

Two articles discuss whether the partner actually stepped back from the engagement during the required five-year cooling-off time.

Final article shows he was lead partner on three more audits.

Be careful of what you say on Facebook

Going Concern picked up on some comments in a Seattle Times article that ran on April 20 (*Missteps marked http://goo.gl/4fl1NRKPMG insider-trading scandal*) which is actually a reprint of the *Los Angeles Times* article which ran on April 11 (*In KPMG insider trading case, crime and blunders alleged*). (http://goo.gl/Xm7E9x) (http://goo.gl/5HKg3k)

The discussion is of comments made by Mr. Scott London on the Facebook page of his golf buddy's wife. The families were close friends. Now even the joking comments made four years ago are subject for examination.

Going Concern's discussion follows their headline – *Scott London Won't Be Making Flirty Comments on the Facebook Page of Bryan Shaw's Wife Anytime Soon.* (http://goo.gl/z084AC)

The *LA Times* article describes the comments. Look up the original article if you are interested):

Moral of the story?

Keep in mind that **anything** you write in a social media platform, anything, could one day appear in the Los Angeles Times. Write your comments accordingly.

Cooling-off time

Francine McKenna explores *KPMG's Insider Trading: What the Auditor, and Skechers, Don't Want To Talk About.* She is trying to understand the sequence of the 'cooling-off' time for Mr. London on the Sketchers audit. (http://goo.gl/S3FvtT)

PCAOB rules require the lead partner to cycle off the audit for 5 years after being the lead partner for 5 years. Best picture she can paint is the cooling-off time ended after he started passing tips to his golf buddy.

She's also tried to get an understanding of his role during the cooling-off time (was he an advisory partner with consulting roles or have a concurring or quality review role?) along with the exact timing of the cooling-off, but hasn't been able to get a clear explanation.

Article has some good background for those of us outside the Big 4 world on how partners and senior managers are rotated between positions.

She also repeats her suggestion from two years ago for disclosure of the full range of partner's involvement with public companies: internal audit, tax, etc. If that were combined with disclosing the concurring partner and actual/standby quality control review partner, there would be a good way to see if a partner had a really good cooling-off time or just stepped back a little bit. Seems to me it is the difference between showing someone actually took a break or stayed involved.

Ms. McKenna expands her discussion in her blog post at re: The Auditors – *Scott London Subverted Sarbanes-Oxley: Big Four Mock Audit Partner Rotation.* (http://goo.gl/LDJ0Jg)

Stepping away from an engagement for five years after that length of time as lead partner seems to make sense to me. Staying involved with the consulting, or tax work, or concurring/quality control partner would seem to seriously undermine that concept. Hmm. I think that's the point of the two articles.

Lead auditor on three more engagements

Financial Times has an article pursing the disclosure of lead partner's name – *Regulator urges end of auditor anonymity.* It just repeats the standard argument for disclosure of lead partner's name. (http://goo.gl/yjmaSM)

Of far more interest to me are these two tidbits, including that he was lead partner on three more audits.

Two privately held companies and one with public debt. I've not seen that comment anywhere else.

Also, this isn't the first time tripping over independence rules. The article says Mr. London didn't disclose timely one/several security trade(s) in 2012.

The article says Mr. London's attorney confirmed he was auditor on three more clients. The attorney also confirmed the minor independence glitch.

Insider trading update 4-24-13 – We should be done with the story by now
4/24/13

The story on a KPMG partner trading on inside information is over.

That is the conclusion from comments by Mr. Michael Andrew, chairman of KPMG International. Mr. Andrew made several noteworthy comments during interviews in China.

The Financial Times reports *KPMG chief dismisses 'one-day wonder' scandal*: (http://goo.gl/u7N9VH)

(This discussion will paraphrase the comments instead of quoting them.)

He said this story is a "one-day wonder."

The reason the story got so much play is there wasn't a whole lot going on the week a regional PIC of a Big 4 firm was indicted on a felony conspiracy charge and sued for insider trading:

He said the level of visibility was because of the slow news week.

Presumably that means the Wall Street Journal editors were bored and just didn't know what to talk about the day they used half the space above the fold on the front page to show a picture of the partner accepting a payoff. For insider trading. In public. With $5,000 provided by the FBI. A second time. (http://goo.gl/NACzpZ)

I'm not that familiar with PCAOB rules, but have a working knowledge of AICPA rules. I was surprised to learn that disclosure of the lead partner's name is prohibited in the U.S.

The executive said confidentiality rules prohibited the firm from mentioning the names of the other three clients.

I asked on Twitter if disclosure was really prohibited and got a response from Big4Veteran saying you could simply go to the annual meeting, shake hands with the partner, and get a business card.

Reuters also has a report from Shanghai: *KPMG chairman says campaign against auditor anonymity misleading.* (Update: link broken.)

In responding to the PCAOB's idea of requiring disclosure of the lead audit partner, Mr. Andrew said doing so wouldn't fix the issues in the audit world that need fixing.

The disclosure lead partner's names would actually be misleading, according to the quote in the article.

I don't think disclosing the name of the lead partner will do any good in terms of improving objectivity and independence. Don't think it would do much harm either. But I can't see how doing so would be misleading.

Of course Going Concern weights in on the slow-news-day comment. Their post *KPMG Global Chairman Doesn't Consider a Partner at His Firm Passing Material Non-public Information About Audit Clients to a Golf Buddy to Be All That Newsworthy* starts with: (http://goo.gl/7WH6Ih)

"I mean, really."

The *Business blog at Financial Times* is a bit more restrained than *Going Concern* (imagine that!): *Too soon for KPMG to come out fighting*:

(http://goo.gl/6BUJJj)

They suggested there may be a time when the executive should go on the attack, but now is not the time. They also suggested he might be less dismissive if he can't stay away from publicity.

What is your price?
4/27/13

We know the price Mr. Scott London, former partner of KPMG is accused of setting for his integrity, honor, and reputation. The entrance price tag was several thousand dollars and added up to under $100,000.

Cumulative amount is allegedly $50K cash plus a watch with claimed FMV of $12K plus some concert tickets for his family, with asserted total around $70K or $90K.

That total allegation isn't the real measure of his price. The starting point was a few thousand dollars in the first deal. If the story outlined in the criminal indictment is correct, that is the point his integrity was sold.

(**Update for book**: The first payment was either $1,000 or $3,000, according to Mr. London. That is the bright-line point at which Mr. London set a firm price.)

An old joke about your price

There is an old joke with many variations that goes something like this:

Man to woman in a social setting: "would you sleep with me for a million dollars?"

She indicated she would be willing to do so.

Him: "How about for $20?"

With great indignation, she said "Of course not! What kind of woman do you think I am?"

Him: "We've already established that. Now we are just haggling over price."

The story is told with a variety of famous men as the inquirer and usually an anonymous woman. Quote Investigator finds the earliest version of the story *in print back in 1937* which puts its first appearance well before the various people to whom it is usually attributed. (http://goo.gl/Y7NAEr)

The point stands.

(**Update**: While the story is a bit off-color, the point applies to all of us. What's our price?)

What is the price of your integrity?

It's a scary question.

One person tested his price point

At some point in my career as auditor the CEO of one of my clients, a rather cynical fellow, said that he knew the price of his integrity was above a certain cutoff. He insisted that everybody had a price at which they *would* compromise their integrity, but most people hadn't been in a situation in which they'd found out the amount.

He indicated he was able to test his price at one point in the past.

There was a situation in which he could have stolen a substantial amount of money and was absolutely certain he knew he could get away without detection and there would be not be any trail. I'm not sure the circumstance, but think we are talking about something like piles of cash sitting on a table with no accountability for the amount.

He walked away from the opportunity. Thus, from his perspective he knows the price of his integrity is higher than the amount of cash involved in that circumstance.

Let's set aside our knowledge of the fraud triangle, especially the idea that severe pressures could change the price point.

His story has stayed with me for a long time.

So here's the question for you:

At what entrance price point would you compromise your integrity and risk your entire future?

What's the price would you set for the first step?

(**Update**: Now that we have the end of the story, we know Mr. London's price. It was the first stack of currency.)

KPMG insider trading fiasco update – how much responsibility does a firm have for ethical failures? – 5-3-13
5/3/13

I've not seen much news lately on the alleged insider trading by former KPMG partner Scott London. Two articles of interest.

These two articles have different perspectives on how much responsibility belongs to the firm. We need a long wrestle match with that question.

A pattern?

Writing at Pacific Coast Business Times, Professor Steven Mintz says in an *Op/ed: KPMG scandal damages reputation of the accounting profession*. (http://goo.gl/IXUEXL)

On one hand, Prof. Mintz is scratching his head like the rest of us who are trying to sort out the motivation. Only thing he can bring to bear is that he quotes the movie Forest Gump about stupidity.

Whether that is the case or not, Prof. Mintz sees a troubling pattern. One incident is difficult enough to process; three dots that seem to be connected are more troublesome.

He sees a possible pattern emerging when he considers this set of allegations, Deloitte and Touche vice chairman Thomas Flanagan sitting in jail for 21 months because of insider trading, and KPMG paying a $456M penalty & seeing three staffers in jail with sentences ranging for 6.5 to 10 years for a tax shelter scandal.

If I'm getting his point, it seems like one partner (Mr. London) with a massive ethical failure is an oddity, but three massive ethical failures (2 at KPMG, 1 at D&T) can't be dismissed so easily.

He closes his op-ed with a discussion that ethical behavior is still the responsibility of the firm.

Good read. Check it out.

Lessons learned for the rest of us

Three litigators from the legal firm of Fried Frank have a column at Mondaq discussing some lessons learned: *Implications of the London/Shaw Insider Trading Case For Public Companies And External Auditors*.

(http://goo.gl/xaACBY)

The first point is the situation doesn't call into question the policies and procedures that KPMG put into place.

The article said that no system of quality control can be strong enough to stop a 'rogue' partner or staff person from passing tips to someone outside the firm's control.

Let me rephrase: What system could prevent or detect a partner who gives a verbal tip to someone outside the firm? Our society would not tolerate the steps necessary to find out what Mr. London is alleged to have done.

Another point from the article is this fiasco should prompt all CPA firms to revisit their independence policies and training. That's a great idea.

If you are wise, you will think about the disasters in your industry and ponder, at least for a moment, "how are we doing on that issue?" I do that all the time when I read about litigation against accountants or see a list of common audit deficiencies.

That fiasco you read about might take only a moment to consider, might take a short conversation, or might prompt a full review. Keep your eyes and ears open for opportunities to improve your firm.

Final implication in the article is labeling as a non sequitur the idea that the alleged behavior of Mr. London means the names of audit partners should be identified. The two issues have nothing to do with each other.

That would be like saying his alleged ethical failure means we should have full adoption of IFRS in the U.S.

Oh, wait. Maybe that non sequitur would improve the arguments in favor of IFRS.

Check out the full article from Fried Frank

Read both articles and ponder how much responsibility a firm has for the ethical behavior of its staff.

2 Responses on my blog:

The Fried Frank thing is stupid. Naming the partner wouldn't help companies or audit firms. They already know who their audit partner is. Naming the partners helps everyone else, including other companies and investors know what other companies are vulnerable to a "rogue". And calling a partner like Flanagan or London a rogue says more about the firm than about them. And why does know one mention Gansman from EY or McClellan and his wife when they talk about vulnerability of firms to tippers at high levels?

Francine McKenna **fmforbes**

May 3, 2013, 11:30 am at 11:30 am

My Reply

I don't think naming the lead partner will do much good.

Your suggestion, or a variation of it, might be useful. Listing *all* the partners on the engagement, including the one signing off on the tax provision, the concurring partner, internal engagement quality control review sign-off (if that's done in the SEC world), and the consulting partners would give a good picture of the team at the senior level. That idea is appealing. Then you could run some intriguing correlations to the companies that seem to be pushing the limit on accounting or have several restatements.

The deeper question, that I can't even explain in a coherent statement, is how does someone like Flanagan or London get to a very senior level? On one hand, how can a firm possibly control the behavior of every person every moment? That's the 'rogue' argument.

On the other hand, shouldn't people at that level have the second-nature attitude of making sure direct reports know they will get thrown out the 35th floor window if they break the law, take a bribe, sleep with a subordinate, or do anything else stupid enough to get the firm on the front page of the *LA Times*? That's 'the firm is responsible' argument.

On the third hand, if it is uncertain whether someone would get fired for that kind of behavior or if the firm allows anarchy, then it is the firm's fault.

Here's an interesting question – - how many partners have been summarily fired for ethical violations? Is that known inside the firms?

I recall a conversation which I'll describe vaguely – a senior level person at one of my clients described a situation when he/she worked at a large company. A person was discovered having committed a serious ethical violation. Said unethical person was fired the next day and everyone in the building knew the real reason even though the for-public-consumption reason was 'seeking other opportunities'. After that day everyone knew that sort of behavior got you thrown out the door. I doubt it happened again.

Oh, thanks for adding two more dots to the three that the professor mentioned – five data points is troubling.

As always, thanks for your comments.

First guilty plea in KPMG insider trading fiasco – 5-7-13 update
5/7/13

On Monday, the Department of Justice indicted Mr. Bryan Shaw, the golfing buddy of former KPMG partner Scott London on one felony count of conspiracy. Mr. Shaw reportedly entered a plea agreement saying he would plead guilty and agree to disgorge about $1.27M of profits.

The press release from the Department of Justice is here.

A few other news reports:
- *Wall Street Journal* – *Guilty Plea in KPMG Case* (http://goo.gl/xFn76p)
- *Los Angeles Times* – *Jeweler agrees to plead guilty in KPMG insider-trading case.* (http://goo.gl/wb6UMY)

I've looked briefly a couple of times and can't find the indictment and plea agreement on-line.

Here are a few comments in the DoJ press release I found interesting. Here's the summary:

Bryan Shaw, 52, of Lake Sherwood, California, was charged this morning in United States District Court with one count of conspiracy. In a plea agreement also filed this morning, Shaw agreed to plead guilty to the felony offense and admitted that he plotted with the former KPMG partner to commit securities fraud. As part of the agreement with federal prosecutors, Shaw agreed to disgorge approximately $1,271,787 in illegal stock trading profits.

More detail on the payments to Mr. London is in the press release. Notice the amount of cash is now "more than $60,000." That is an increase of the previously reported amount, but not by a lot.

Shaw admits in his plea agreement that he gave London more than $60,000 in cash in exchange for confidential information about KPMG's clients, typically meeting with London near Shaw's Encino jewelry store to give him bags containing stacks of $100 bills. Shaw also admits in his plea agreement that he gave London a $12,000 Rolex Daytona Cosmograph watch, as well as jewelry and concert tickets, in exchange for the confidential information.

The penalty can include double the gain from the insider trading. That could expose Mr. London to a $2.5M disgorgement, but I don't know if the Feds do a double counting on the disgorgement issue:

The federal charge of conspiracy to commit securities fraud carries a statutory maximum penalty of five years in prison, and a fine of $250,000 or twice the gross gain or loss from the offense.

Not much new since the story first broke yesterday. Next major news will be court appearances by Mr. Shaw this week and by Mr. London on 5-17.

Update on court appearances for players in KPMG insider trading fiasco
5/16/13

The *Agoura Hills Patch* reports *Businessman Out on Bail in KPMG Insider Trading Case Involving Agoura Hills Man*. (http://goo.gl/eUEXqR)

I've been watching for news on these court appearances and no one else seems to have given any coverage.

The article says Bryan Shaw was in court last Friday, 5/10. He is out on $50,000 bail with his next court appearance on Monday 5/20. He is expected to enter a guilty plea.

Scott London will appear in court on Thursday, May 30. Initially he was going to appear Friday, May 17.

Bryan Shaw pleads guilty for conspiracy in KPMG insider trading fiasco because he's guilty. Oh, and a really small additional consequence for Mr. London – #8
5/20/13

The tippee in the KPMG insider trading case, Bryan Shaw, entered a guilty plea Monday on one count.

Check out the identical headlines (no, they aren't from the same reporter or picked up on from a wire service):

- The *Los Angeles Times* reports in *Jeweler pleads guilty in KPMG insider-trading case*. (http://goo.gl/LsTCkx)
- The *Wall Street Journal* reports in *Jeweler Pleads Guilty in KPMG Insider-Trading Case* (http://goo.gl/Wmp1Wq)

Sentencing is set for September 16.

Why did he plead guilty? Because he is.

Check out the very unlawyerly like comment from his lawyer. Mr. Shaw is guilty so that is why he is pleading guilty. The attorney says Mr. Shaw has been saying he made decisions that were incredibly stupid.

Mr. London will be in court May 30, which is Thursday of next week.

Note: Consequence discussed in this post moved to the consequence chapter.

Former KPMG partner enters plea agreement
5/29/13

Former KPMG regional audit PIC Scott London entered a plea agreement on Tuesday according to multiple media sources.

The agreement says he passed information to his golf buddy at least 14 times.

The *Encino Patch* article linked below says he will plead guilty to one felony charge of securities fraud through insider trading with potential prison term of 20 years. Multiple other reports list that as the potential penalty. *The Week* adds that the potential fine is up to $5M. (http://goo.gl/aMbRUI)

The article also says Mr. London likely won't be appearing in court this Friday, as was previously scheduled.

I can't find the plea agreement on-line. Published reports about the plea don't show any new information that wasn't previously known.

(**Update**: Plea and other documents will be linked later in the book.)

Mr. Shaw is expected to be sentenced September 16.

A few articles for further info:

- *Encino-Tarzana Patch* – *Accountant Pleads Guilty to Securities Fraud* (http://goo.gl/wZB6I7)
- *Wall Street Journal* – *Former KPMG Partner Agrees to Plead Guilty in Insider-Trading Scheme.* (http://goo.gl/145qVE)

As of this morning, there isn't a press release posted at the website for the U.S. Attorney for Central District of California.

Update: The U.S. Attorney's press release is here. Only new information is that Mr. London will appear in court June 17 for arraignment.

Former KPMG partner in court for arraignment and procedural issues; on camera interview with CNBC
6/17/13

Scott London was in court today on procedural matters regarding the criminal complaint alleging insider trading.

CNBC has a video interview with him. (http://goo.gl/th5bQL)

The *Wall Street Journal* and *Los Angeles Times* have more details.

A few tidbits from the televised interview...

He estimates the amount he received is about $70. That would be $50K of cash, a watch he was told is worth about $10K, and 3 or 4 other pieces of jewelry he recently had appraised for just under $10k.

That makes about $70K. No mention of the concert tickets in the interview.

He insisted nothing like this has happened before.

Slippery slope

Here is the first info I've seen on how this developed:

The partial info in the video and printed article suggests there was a slippery slope. Started with complaining about things over dinner. You know how that goes, "those guys messed up my plans for Saturday 'cause they are gonna' announce ...." Then Mr. Shaw started trading. My guess is after some amount of trading Mr. Shaw gave Mr. London some money. Obviously the first few amounts were apparently accepted. The sharing of info continued. The cash continued.

That is part info from the interview, part from the text of the article, and part my guess. Hope we hear more details.

Amount of gains

He thought that Mr. Shaw had only made about $200k.

His reaction when he found out that the profits were about $1.3M? According to the print report he was extremely upset, to the point of being nauseated. He though Mr. Shaw had made about $200k in profits.

That's an odd response. I'm not sure why there would be increased distress from knowing the gains were around $1.3M instead of $0.2M. He would have found out that information after he had decided to confess. He would have already known he was going to jail.

Why do you think he was that much more upset?

What's next?

He said he will get past this and get back to work since he has two children to put through college.

Court appearance

The *Wall Street Journal* reports *KPMG Ex-Partner is Arraigned*. (http://goo.gl/i0xfFY)

The *Los Angeles Times* reports *Arraignment postponed for ex-KPMG auditor in insider-trading case*. (http://goo.gl/SgOK1G)

Procedural things took place today.

A formal plea of not guilty was entered. A change will take place later, I think. The case will be transferred to the judge handling Mr. Shaw's case. Boundaries of the travel restriction have been expanded. He wanted to turn over the jewelry but the appropriate agents who could accept the jewelry were not available.

As I post this, there are only those three reports visible from an internet search.

Update: Pursing the case as only Going Concern can do, we can follow up on the comment on waiting tables in the interview: *Let's Ponder Scott London's Potential Future in the Service Industry*. (http://goo.gl/EsMPjl)

Another interview with admitted inside-trader from KPMG
7/11/13

Scott London has given another interview, this time with the Agora Hills Acorn – *Community leader's fall from grace stemmed from insider trading*. (http://goo.gl/SkSs96)

If you are really interested in the former KPMG partner's story, you'll want to check out the article.

Here's a few interesting tidbits with my observations:

The insider work ran for about 16 months when Mr. London and his golf buddy, Bryan Shaw, mutually decided to end it, according to the article.

The article expands the developing narrative that passing on insider info started slowly and just grew over time. On one hand, you might think that makes it sound a bit more innocent. On the other hand, that tells me there would have been many opportunities to say 'stop.'

After a break, the conversations and info sharing resumed when the FBI wired Mr. Shaw for a sting operation. Seems to me that again provided opportunities to say 'knock it off.'

The article says Mr. London says Mr. Shaw said the illicit proceeds would be split three ways, between Mr. Shaw, Mr. London, and the taxman.

That would be why Mr. London thought the $50K plus watch would imply that Mr. Shaw had made around $200K. (50K cash + ~10K/12K watch = ~60K ; ~60K / 3 = ~180K ; ~180K rounds to ~200K).

Mr. London presumably didn't audit (or review or compile) Mr. Shaw's trading profits, so it makes sense Mr. London thought the proceeds were about 200K.

That answers the question I had about why Mr. London was so shocked the proceeds were around $1.3M instead of $200K.

The article says his family and friends have stood by him. I'm glad for that.

Minor updates on insider trading fiasco at KPMG – 9-10-13
9/10/13

Only a little news lately as we wait for sentencing of confessed insider traders. Latest I've seen is that Scott London will receive his sentence on October 21 and Bryan Shaw on September 16.

Here are two articles I've noticed:

8-3 – *Spy team is Wall Street regulator's weapon against insider traders – Gnom.es National News Service* – Update: Link is broken but article was picked up by *LA Times.*

Background article on FINRA's electronic monitoring of trades to search for insider trading.

FINRA is the organization that discovered insider trading by Scott London and Bryan Shaw.

They are the Financial Industry Regulatory Authority, a part of Wall Street that provides self-regulation. They are the successor to NASD. They have no enforcement power, so they turn over their information to federal agencies for further investigation.

The article shows they have lots of trade data and more importantly have the ability to sift through it to find oddities.

9-6 – *Venture County sheriff takes aim at rouge doctors, pharmacists* – *Pacific Coast Business Times* (http://goo.gl/98F4KD)

Another consequence for Mr. London – his name is a reference point for describing the severity of criminal investigations.

Ventura County sheriff has a Pharma Task Force looking at prescription drug abuse in the 101 corridor running from Camarillo to Westlake Village. The suspicion is there are a number of doctors and a few pharmacies that are putting thousands of addictive prescription drugs on the street. The task force has made a few arrests.

The end of the article links this to a string of high visibility bad-news stories in Conejo Valley, including the insider trading of Scott London and Brian Shaw. After describing their mess, the article describes their arrests as a "thunderbolt" in the valley. The shock waves from the few arrests so far in the pharma investigation are described as not quite as sharp as those from the London-Shaw fiasco.

Picture the conversation next year. Breathless lead reporter racing into editor's office: "Hey boss, we got another London here, maybe bigger than London!" Editor yells, "hold the presses!"

How sad – Mr. London provides a frame of reference for DAs and reporters.

Update - Full disclosure – I haven't mentioned it in a while, but I worked for KPMG a long time ago, in the distant past when it was called Peat, Marwick, Mitchell.

Who first discovered the KPMG insider trading mess?
9/12/13

Who should get credit for discovering the insider trading by KPMG former partner Scott London and his golfing buddy, Brian Shaw?

That's the question raised by a reader, Gary Zeune, after I posted this article yesterday: *Minor updates on insider trading fiasco at KPMG.* (http://goo.gl/2CpOvm)

I think the answer is FINRA.

FINRA's involvement

This article, *Spy_team is Wall Street regulator's weapon against insider traders*, suggests it was FINRA who first noticed the unusual trading and then turned that information over to other parties. (Update: link broken)

FINRA can only do research and then turn over their info to the appropriate law enforcement agency. The article says FINRA doesn't have any subpoena power, so they pass their information on to the appropriate federal agency.

Earlier in the article, there is a comment that the Assistant U.S. Attorney said info from FINRA lead to the arrests.

Fidelity Investment's involvement

Mr. Zeune recollected that Fidelity Investment first identified the fraud. That comment did ring a bell.

I did a word search on the SEC charges (available here) and the federal indictment (available here) and quickly browsed both documents. I didn't notice any mention of either Fidelity or FINRA as the source. Maybe I missed it.

The published reports I have on hand mention that Fidelity freezing the account was the first sign to Mr. London and Mr. Shaw that the feds might be on to them. Here are two comments:

Wall Street Journal - *Secret Recordings, Cash in Insider Sting* says in July 2012 Fidelity Brokerage Services froze the account of Mr. Shaw. That is from the criminal information charge filed. Fidelity had nothing to say about a client's account, obviously. (http://goo.gl/ihJXfg)

Los Angeles Times – *In KPMG insider trading case, crime and blunders alleged* says Mr. Shaw kept trading after the account was frozen. (http://goo.gl/oZnn83)

Both reports use neutral verbs and don't specify who first noticed the suspicious trading. They just identify that Fidelity froze the account.

Freezing the account produced Mr. London's comment comparing insider trading to card counting in Vegas. From page 13 of the indictment (link above):

"Shaw said that LONDON reassured him that there was no reason for concern, and explained that insider trading was like counting cards at a casino in Las Vegas – if you were caught, they simply ask you to leave because they cannot prove it."

Mr. London was quite wrong on the insider trading idea and I'm guessing the casinos can do far more than just walk you to the door.

Sequence

So the sequence isn't quite clear, but putting the pieces together suggests FINRA noticed the trading first. There are some not-yet-disclosed additional steps between FINRA's discovery and Fidelity's freezing the account. Presumably the SEC and perhaps other agencies were involved. My guess, based on mere recollection, is the FBI got involved late fall/early winter, well after the brokerage account was frozen.

At some point I'd like to piece together more of the puzzle and write in more detail. Stay tuned for more.

Update: I identified Mr. Zeune as the reader who asked the question. Thanks for asking. Anyone have more info to help answer the question?

Additional update: After further reading, I'm not quite so sure FINRA get the credit. See next post for follow-up.

2 Responses to the post:

It was FINRA that noticed the Deloitte's Flanagan insider trading issues based on his trading in M&A targets. The other clients were M&A related activity unlike Skechers and Herbalife. So there's some reason to believe FINRA is on the job these days.

Francine McKenna (@retheauditors)

Reply

Francine:

I hope that is the case. Even better would be if everyone knew that FINRA was looking at trade level information.

Thanks for the comment.

Jim

Update on wondering who first discovered the KPMG insider trading mess
9/20/13

I previously concluded that FINRA, the self-regulatory branch of the securities industry, gets credit for discovering the insider trading scam involving a now-former senior level partner at KPMG.

Now, I'm not so sure.

By the way, we are still waiting for sentencing of Mr. Shaw. I've been watching the news closely but nothing has been visible this week. Back to the main question -

Gary Zeune and I have briefly looked at some more of the public reporting on the fiasco. After doing so, neither of us are sure whether it was FINRA or Fidelity that first found the illegal trading.

My previous post concluded FINRA first found the trading. That post quoted an article that initially appeared in the *Los Angeles Times* on July 30, 2013. (http://goo.gl/xdGiPG)

Here are a few articles that hint the trading may have been found by the brokerage firm holding the account where the trades were executed.

The *Los Angeles Times* reported on May 20, 2013, *Jeweler pleads guilty in KPMG insider-trading case*: that Fidelity Investments seemed to identify the suspicious trading with the speculation attributed to Mr. Shaw's attorney. (http://goo.gl/zPq3dz)

CTV News, *Ex-KPMG partner pleads guilty in insider trading case*, comments the brokerage firm call the FBI and SEC. (http://goo.gl/6Zk9o4)

Could be that freezing the account is just the first sign the duo saw that the feds were on to them. The *Wall Street Journal's* says on April 11, 2013, *Secret Recordings, Cash in Insider Sting*, the first indications something was wrong was when the account was frozen. (http://goo.gl/2eEWui)

Those three newspaper reports could be what was publicly known at the time and could also just reflect what was known by the defense team. FINRA's involvement prior to Fidelity's freezing of the accounts would likely have been invisible at the time.

So, it's not quite clear who first tumbled to the trading by Mr. London and Mr. Shaw. The higher likelihood is FINRA, but I'm not as sure as I was a few days ago. Guess that just shows that fraud is murky.

Ex-KPMG partner banned from practice before the SEC; sentencing date is in December
9/30/13

The SEC banned KPMG's former regional audit PIC Scott London from SEC related work. The key sentence from Bloomberg's article *SEC Bars Former KPMG Partner for Role in Insider-Trading Scheme* says Mr. London is banned as an accountant for any public company. (http://goo.gl/U7V2UR)

Another article is Market Watch: *KPMG's Scott London barred for insider trading*. (http://goo.gl/E4gRSz)

The Bloomberg article says Mr. London will be sentenced on December 9, 2013.

This is an update from the latest info I'd seen, which was for sentencing to be October 21.

Previous visible date for sentencing of Bryan Shaw was September 16; but that date has past without any visible indication sentencing took place.

Update: See *Sentencing in London CPA insider trading case set for 2-27-14*. (http://goo.gl/XPSQEQ)

Sentencing watch

Sentencing recommendation and suggestion for lighter sentence for ex-KPMG partner's insider trading
10/21/13

Going Concern has breaking news about the KPMG insider trading fiasco. They have a copy of the court filing by Mr. Scott London taking exception to the pre-sentencing report from the United States Probation Office.

Check out *Reminder: Insider Trading Turned Out Badly for Ex-KPMG Partner Scott London*. (http://goo.gl/TShUZa)

The GC copy of the filing can be found here. (http://goo.gl/4rgOk1)

I will have more to say about the case after the sentencing. Here are a few initial thoughts on the filing.

Arguments for shorter sentence – amounts involved

The pre-sentencing report (which I now know is called a PSR) called for downgrading to a 36 month sentence from what is calculated from federal guidelines as a 46 to 57 month range.

Mr. London's attorney argues it should be in the recommended range of 18 to 24 months based on the amount involved that Mr. London would reasonably have expected to be involved.

The filing spells out in the analytical detail you would expect from a CPA why Mr. London reasonably believed the amount of Mr. Shaw's illicit gains were about $200K. Specifically:

- Mr. Shaw indicated he would use one-third of the proceeds to pay his taxes (Mr. London assumed a 30% rate instead).
- The remaining proceeds would be split between Mr. Shaw and Mr. London, according to Mr. London's recollection.
- Mr. London received approximately $66,000 of cash and tangible items (thus confirming the public reports suggesting proceeds were in the 50k/60k range).
- Thus, backing up Mr. London's ~$66K net proceeds to Mr. Shaw's gross proceeds means Mr. London believed Mr. Shaw grossed about $200K.

That explains publicly visible comments of shock by Mr. London when he heard the amounts involved were over $1M.

Therefore, Mr. London's filing argues the sentencing should be based on a $200K amount instead of $1.27M. That would knock the calculated range down from 46-58 months to 18-24 months. I am guessing a further down-grade for voluntary cooperation and no previous record would reduce that further.

Scheme ended before the investigation started

Another factor Mr. London takes exception to in the PSR asserting the scheme would have continued without federal intervention. He asserts the scheme ended in April 2012.

The only reason there was more info passed on by Mr. London in early 2013 was that Mr. Shaw was pushing the issue *after* the investigation started at the insistence of the FBI. From the filing:

"It should be noted that Mr. London, after a great deal of prodding on the part of Shaw, who at this point was taking part in the "sting operation" that led to Mr. London's arrest, did give Shaw a final tip in or around early February of 2013. This only occurred after considerable badgering from Mr. Shaw. "

Walk away

One of the first lessons from this is if someone suggests breaking the law, DON'T.

A lesson I've mentioned previously: If your friend-you-didn't-know-was-trading-on-inside-information pushes a wad of cash across the table to you, shut your mouth, stand up, and WALK AWAY.

Today's lesson is that if you have stopped breaking the law and your friend-in-crime insists on starting up again, DON'T.

If said friend-who-is-not-a-friend insists on handing you another stack of cash in a parking lot, shut your mouth, turn around, and WALK AWAY.

There are so many places where Mr. London could have stopped this travesty.

If he had wanted to. That's a big IF.

Final arguments for lighter sentence –
fine too high and cooperation provided

The filing also suggests a $100K fine is excessive. Really?

More reasonable would be $25K, according to the filing.

Final reason the filing says the proposed sentence is too high is it did not give sufficient credit for the assistance Mr. London gave KPMG to mitigate the impact on the firm.

The filing cites the damage caused to Arthur Andersen after Enron as a reason Mr. London was so quick to fully disclose to KPMG his actions and to cooperate with them. He wanted to prevent serious trauma to the firm.

Interesting tidbits are that Mr. London had to get permission from the US Attorney before he disclosed the existence of the investigation to the firm.

If you are interested, you can read the Going Concern article. If you are really, really interested, the link to the court filing is above.

There's much more to say. I'll pull things together after the sentencing hearings.

Sentencing dates for KPMG insider trading case
10/23/13

An article in the *Los Angeles Times* reports *KPMG auditor deserves 3 years for insider trading, probation office says*. (http://goo.gl/W9SNeG)

The article covers the same ground broken by *Going Concern* here, which I discussed. New information is the expected sentencing dates. (http://goo.gl/TShUZa)

The Times article says Mr. London will be sentenced on 12-9-13. Mr. Shaw will be sentenced on 1-23-14.

Won't be a particularly festive holiday season for either of them. Another earned consequence for both their families.

Sentencing in London CPA insider trading case set for 2-27-14
1/30/14

Docket for Scott I. London's case for insider trading shows the sentencing hearing has been moved to 2/27/14. Sentencing position papers due by 2/13/14.

Case number 2:13-cr-00379-GW (I'm just learning to ride this bicycle, so that may or may not be the right citation). Or maybe it's 2:13-mj-01058-DUTY.

Admissions in Scott London's plea agreement: felony insider trading 14 times
2/6/14

Have you ever read a federal plea agreement for an individual? I've read court documents for criminal cases from the county where I live and civil cases at the federal level. This is the first individual criminal case from the federal level. Wow!

I just subscribed to the PACER system, which provides access to public documents in the federal court system. I'm still learning how to ride that bicycle. Looks like it will be quite useful.

One of the first things I looked at is the case of Mr. Scott London, most recently a senior level partner at KPMG, in charge of the southwest regional audit practice. As I've mentioned on this blog, he has pled guilty to insider trading.

The plea agreement is amazing. The phrasing is rather harsh and the admissions are exquisitely clear. I'll share some of the things I noticed in this public document.

Admissions

In the written agreement, Mr. London admits he is guilty of insider trading and admits all the facts in Exhibit A. The exhibit is written in a rather heavy-handed way. But Mr. London agreed. In writing.

By signing the agreement, he admits that between about October 2010 and about May 2012 he

"knowingly and willfully engaged in a conspiracy … to commit securities fraud through insider trading."

Wow. No wiggle room there.

He admits to passing on information about each of the following SEC registered clients of KPMG:

- Herbalife
- Skechers
- Deckers Outdoor Corporation
- Pacific Capital Bancorp - acquired by UnionBanCal
- RSC Holdings, Inc. – acquired by United Rentals, Inc.

Mr. London admits he provided confidential insider information to Mr. Shaw knowing Mr. Shaw would trade on the information.

Mr. London admits to passing inside information at least 14 times. Four specific incidents are explained in detail.

I think that means he admits, in writing, to 14 felonies. I suppose there could be more.

Other stray terms

Some items in the agreement are quite strong. I can't imagine what the supervised release terms look like.

Mr. London agrees he will not contest any of the facts in the agreement.

He agrees not to seek discharge of any restitution order in bankruptcy. Not a big deal in this case but that could be a *really* big deal for someone hit with tens or hundreds of millions of dollars of disgorgement in a big Wall Street case.

The plea agreement reminds Mr. London that after the felony conviction he loses

- the right to vote,
- the right to possess a firearm or ammunition,
- the right to hold office, and
- the right to sit on a jury.

It will be a felony to merely possess ammunition.

He agrees he will not appeal the conviction or reasonableness of the fine or the sentence. He will accept any terms imposed by the judge.

Something in London case about to go under seal
2/13/14

Just checking to see if anything new is showing up on a couple of cases I'm following in the federal PACER system.

Sentencing arguments were due to the court on 2/13/14 in the case of Scott London, lately a senior partner at KPMG. He was the regional audit PIC prior to getting his picture on the front page of the *Wall Street Journal* during an FBI recorded cash-for-inside-information payment.

On 2/13/14, the Assistant US Attorney filed an ex parte motion to place something under seal. The document description is "other" and the reason is "under seal." Setting aside my severely limited knowledge of law and using my businessman's understanding instead, I think that means the documents will be under seal and the reason it will be nonpublic is under seal.

My very wild guess on the contents is based on the filing taking place on the day the sentencing positions were due. My guess? The sealed document is the sentencing argument from the feds.

Your guess?

Sentencing watch for insider trading case
2/24/14

Sentencing is scheduled for former KPMG regional audit PIC Scott London on February 27, 2014 regarding his plea agreement admitting insider trading. That's the latest visible information in the federal system that shows filings.

Previous post mentioned on 2/13 that *Something in London case about to go under seal.*

On 2/18 there were four documents filed under seal. Obviously the contents of those filings aren't visible on the PACER system. My completely wild, uneducated guess would be those are arguments from the defense and prosecution about sentencing. Could also be recommendations from the federal group that provides sentencing guidance to judges.

If you are really interested, keep your eyes open on Thursday. If you are only slightly interested, check back here. I'll keep you updated.

The suspense and wait continues –
Scott London sentencing for insider trading
rescheduled from February 27 to April 21
2/25/14

Since there has been so much traffic today checking out posts about the scheduled date for Scott London's sentencing for his admitted insider trading (thank you for the mention, Going Concern!), I thought to check the federal document system before turning in for the night.

Guess what I found?

The sentencing has been continued from February 27 to April 21.

Previously mentioned there were four documents filed under seal.

As of yesterday morning, all four entries had a date of 2/18/2014 and said:

> "SEALED DOCUMENT- Under Seal Document (mat) (Entered: 02/19/2014)"

When I looked a few minutes ago, item #45 still had a date of 2/18/2014 but the comment has been changed. It now reads:

> "SEALED DOCUMENT- Under Seal Document – Sentencing hearing set for 02/27/14, continued to 04/21/14 at 8:00 a.m. (mat) Modified on 2/24/2014 (jag). (Entered: 02/19/2014)"

That means the sentencing which had previously been scheduled for February 27 has now been moved to April 21, 2014.

Everyone who had been looking forward to a generous serving of popcorn and schadenfreude on Thursday will have to wait another 2 months.

Update: According to the comments on the docket, sentencing has been continued to the following dates: 10/21/13, 12/9/13, 1/27/14, 2/6/14, 2/27/14, and 4/21/14.

Other tidbits: Passport was surrendered on 4/17/13. Turned in $50K on 4/19/13, which is presumably the estimated proceeds of the then-alleged insider trading.

Update July 2014: the $50K was part of the $150K bond posted to avoid jail. It was held until incarceration, at which point on request of Mr. London, the judge ordered it to be applied to the judgment penalty.

Scott London surrendered his CPA license
in December 2013
2/26/14

California Board of Accountancy's Update #74, sent by email this morning, had the following news:

(Following text is quoted from CBA's newsletter)

58

LONDON, SCOTT IAN
Agoura Hills, CA (CPA 46174)
CBA ACTIONS
Surrender of CPA license, via stipulated settlement.

Mr. London shall pay the CBA its costs of investigation and prosecution in the amount of $1,637.50 prior to issuance of a new or reinstated license.

Effective December 27, 2013
CAUSE FOR DISCIPLINE
Accusation No. AC-2014-10 contains the following allegations:

On or about July 1, 2013, Mr. London was convicted of one count of securities fraud through insider trading, in violation of Title 15, United States Code, Sections 78j(b), and 78ff and Title 17, Code of Federal Regulations, Section 240.10b-5 pursuant to a plea agreement.

The circumstances underlying the criminal conviction are that Mr. London, a senior partner at the accounting firm KPMG, LLP, knowingly and willfully engaged in a conspiracy to commit securities fraud through insider trading with his friend. Mr. London would provide material, non-public information (inside information) regarding certain publicly-traded KPMG clients to his friend in violation of the fiduciary and other duties of trust and confidence that Mr. London owed to KPMG and its clients, knowing his friend would make securities transactions based on that inside information. Mr. London received cash payments as compensation for providing the inside information regarding KPMG's clients.

Mr. London's actions that resulted in the conviction also constitute acts of unprofessional conduct involving dishonesty or fraud and breach of fiduciary responsibility.

VIOLATION(S) CHARGED
Business and Professions Code, Division 1.5, Chapter 3, § 490; Division 3, Chapter 1, §§ 5100(a), (c) and (i). California Code of Regulations, Title 16, Division 1, § 99.

(End of extended quote)

I requested permission from the California Board of Accountancy for permission to reprint the above information and was advised by a representative that since disciplinary actions are public documents, permission is not needed.

Just wanted to disclose my request. The material is obviously written by the CBA and is used with their knowledge, even if permission isn't needed.

Loss of license

That stipulation means Mr. London agreed to surrender his license with an effective date of 12/27/13. Not a pleasant holiday for him or his family. Especially since the sentencing date for the criminal case kept getting pushed back a few weeks at a time through the holidays.

Update #74 can be found here. (http://goo.gl/x1bNqE)

The disciplinary action can be found here. (http://goo.gl/EVPexZ)

Full disclosure: For anyone who didn't know, the California Board of Accountancy is the regulatory agency with oversight authority of my CPA practice.

KPMG global chairman speaks about insider trading fiasco
3/8/14

John Veihmeyer, U.S. and global chairman of KPMG, addressed the Scott London insider trading mess during a speaking event with the University of Richmond's Robins School of Business on Tuesday evening, March 4.

I found coverage of his discussion in two media outlets:
- *Richmond Times-Dispatch* – *KPMG top executive reflects on difficult choices in Richmond talk* (http://goo.gl/93aO1l)
- *The Collegian*, University of Richmond student newspaper – *KPMG chairman speaks at fireside chat.* (Update: link broken)

I will paraphrase a number of comments. The Times-Dispatch article said Mr. Veihmeyer decided to fire Mr. London the day he heard. That was a Friday. On the following Monday, he told the leadership team to have a press release available by the end of the day. The firm also withdrew audit opinions on two clients.

The article then quotes Mr. Veihmeyer explaining the firm had to make difficult decisions without all the information at hand. Sometimes you have to make your best call amongst a variety of bad options. Which is least bad?

Article then says Mr. Veihmeyer emailed every employee of the firm a copy of the criminal complaint.

Here's some guidance on how to look at organizations from the outside when something goes horribly wrong. I find the concept has tremendous value in many situations. The best way to measure the attitude of an organization is not whether nothing every goes wrong. That is going to happen. The way to evaluate an organization is what it does when it finds out something went wrong.

Maybe you couldn't do anything to prevent a bad situation developing. It is possible to get blindsided. The issue is what do you do when the situation hits you. How do you handle it?

I've applied that concept on several audits. Something came up that was the duty of senior leadership or the board to address.

Presenting their issue to them allowed me to watch their reaction. How the people dealt with their situation showed me their priorities and values. On more than one occasion I've been able to observe my clients' integrity in real time.

(**Update**: As I ponder those comments during editing, I realize that is a variation of Mr. London's comment that his quick confession revealed his core, or real, personality. You may disagree with either or both of Mr. Veihmeyer's and Mr. London's comments if you wish. The point stands that how you respond in a crunch tells others a lot about you.)

Timing

Let me rephrase the comments from Mr. Veihmeyer on the timing.

The situation broke on a Friday; that's when he learned of the investigation of Mr. London.

He decided to fire Mr. London that day.

On the following Monday he told his team to prepare and issue a press release that same day.

In the same paragraph, the article says KPMG decided to withdraw from two audits. The article doesn't say which day that decision was made.

Mr. London was charged during that same week. When KPMG got hold of the criminal complaint, it was sent out to every employee of the firm.

The Collegian article gave different details on a few key points, which I will paraphrase and then parse. When the information hit the firm's office, there was a choice to be made about how fast to address the issue through a long careful investigation or not.

They addressed the issue head on.

The article says by Monday morning, Mr. Veihmeyer had decided to have KPMG get news out. On Monday morning, his team has a list of tasks to complete by 4 that afternoon. Someone on the staff said they would have more time than that because the news wouldn't be breaking by then.

Mr. Veihmeyer indicated it would be KPMG that made the info public by then.

Releasing news that bad before it comes out some other way is an assertive way to deal with a disaster.

People who study crisis management will have time over the next few years to dissect the moment-by-moment decision-making. In the meantime, that is a good lesson for all of us on how to take charge of a mess and deal with it.

The blog Going Concern has a discussion as well. I picked up on the story from their article, *John Veihmeyer Not at All Ashamed to Talk Scott London to Business School*. (http://goo.gl/8iJ5JU)

By the way, here's another minor consequence for Mr. London – watch how Adrienne Gonzalez has redefined his name.

> "If you recall, an anonymous KPMG insider wrote a piece for us last year just after the Scott hit the fan and talked about how that very response from the firm felt like just what he wanted from the firm."

Please remember that links to articles on the internet have a short URL at the end of the paragraph linking to the article. For example:

(http://goo.gl/yjh2rb)

In addition, live links are available at the publisher's web site. You can find the live links at:

http://riverstonefinancepress.com/tragedy-links/

London Sentencing

Sentencing position papers filed with court in
Scott London insider trading case
4/8/14

The U.S. Attorney and Scott London both filed their sentencing position papers on April 7. This is in advance of the sentencing, expected this month.

Mr. London will file his sentencing position brief under seal, according to a filing from his attorney. That means we won't be reading his arguments, as presented in the filing, anytime soon.

The government's filing mentions there will be a sentencing hearing on April 21, 2014 at 8:00 a.m. That means that as of 4/7, the hearing is still set for 4/21, as previously mentioned in court filings.

The US Attorney is recommending 3 years in prison, 3 years supervised release, and a $100,000 fine. (There's also a $100 special assessment. I have no idea {yet} what that is for.)

Prison term

The government recommendation is 36 months in prison. This is also the recommendation of the federal probation officer.

Federal sentencing guidelines point toward a term of 46 to 57 months. That is mitigated by Mr. London accepting responsibility immediately, his lack of previous criminal record, and having previously led an exemplary life. The filing also acknowledges Mr. London has "serious collateral punishment" for the crime.

The filing spends a few pages arguing against Mr. London's position that only the foreseeable gains should enter into the sentencing calculation, not the total amount of actual proceeds.

The difference of his thinking that there was $200K of gains versus the actual gains of $1.27M makes a big difference in the sentencing calculation. The government filing quotes a variety of sources, all of which seem to be making the point that it is the total haul, not what you knew about, that enters into sentencing guidelines.

A few comments on this being a minor incident – the filing says:

"Thus, this is not a "mistake" or a "lapse in judgment." This was a calculated and corrupt arrangement – - one that generated approximated $70,000 in secret profits to defendant and more than $1 million in proceeds to Shaw."

One argument in support of that idea is the government's characterization that Mr. London seemed unconcerned about resuming the scheme at Mr. Shaw's prodding. We know that request came at the request of the FBI and those conversations were recorded. The discussions weren't along the lines of something like "yeah, they'll do okay this quarter", but were in fact quite detailed in terms of results, and the likely impact on stock prices. The government alleges that Mr. London said, on tape, something about there will be more opportunities for them to make money.

(**Update during editing for book**: I'm going to spend very little time cross-referencing comments in different posts. A detailed analysis is for later. Maybe. However, note the difference between the fed's comment that Mr. London wasn't hesitant to resume the scheme compared to Mr. London's comment in his 4 hour interview that Mr. London brushed off a number of insistent requests from Mr. Shaw before giving in.)

An interesting tidbit in the government filing says that probation would send a message that insider trading isn't serious. I can't tell if that reference to probation is a straw man or actually rebutting an argument that is in play. My guess is for the straw man option – if it were a serious argument, then it seems to me there would be pages of rather strong rebuttal. (*See update below*)

Trust and reputation are
neither an internal control nor a mitigating factor

In the audit world, CPAs often say trust is not an internal control. On the contrary, having an extremely high level of trust is a prerequisite for handing cash, and especially payroll records. Trusting your bookkeeper is a minimum skill to do the job.

The government filing (p 22) acknowledges many letters of support from Mr. London's friends, acquaintances, and colleagues. Those letters describe a diligent, hard-working accountant who had great trust from his colleagues. The filing argues that trust creates a higher responsibility to protect confidential information and is not a mitigating factor.

Ironically, it is that extremely high trust that KPMG, its clients, and Mr. London's colleagues had in him that enabled him to have access to the information on which he committed insider trading.

As for the serious collateral consequences, the filing points out those are the direct results of Mr. London's individual choice of action.

Restitution and fine

The government filing indicates the KPMG has not requested restitution. Thus restitution is not part of the sentencing. Public comments from KPMG indicate that will take place through civil litigation.

Federal guidelines indicate a fine of between $10k and $100k is indicated, according to the filing. The government argues for $100K on the basis that fines are designed to be punitive and the presentencing report indicates he has the ability to pay that amount.

The L.A. Times has a brief story today: *KPMG auditor should get 3 years for insider trading, prosecutors say*. (http://goo.gl/wQbdcR)

Update: Oops. The filing by Mr. London actually did request probation. I missed references to that in my reading of the government's filing. Several minor typos and grammar errors were corrected in this post.

Scott London asked for probation for insider trading
4/9/14

Michael Rapoport reports yesterday in the Wall Street Journal on the sentencing filings: *U.S. Attorney Asks Judge for Three Year Sentence for Former KPMG Partner*. (http://goo.gl/q3ODs9)

I discussed this in the previous post.

Almost bruised my jaw when it hit the keyboard after reading the sentence that said Mr. London's attorney requested probation - no jail time.

Probation. Really? Yes.

That paragraph continues with quoting Mr. Braun from an interview on Tuesday.

How did I miss that when reading the government's probation recommendation?

Check out Mr. Rapoport's article for yourself to make sure I didn't misread it. I previously mentioned Mr. London's response to the presentencing report (PSR) here: *Sentencing recommendation and suggestion for lighter sentence for ex-KPMG partner's insider trading*. (http://goo.gl/NnBC5w)

Since writing that post, I've gained access to the federal filings, available through the PACER program.

The government's filing contains this comment on page 7:

"While the **probationary sentence requested by defendant** is too lenient and would not adequately reflect the seriousness of his crime and would undermine general deterrence, (emphasis added)"

Last night I read through Mr. London's 9/23/13 response to the PSR. It actually does not take a position on the appropriate sentencing. What it does is take exception to the probation officer's methodology which concluded the proper sentencing guideline would be 46-57 months with downward variance to 36 months. That filing is essentially saying the starting point for sentencing was too high, by about 10 'levels' in the federal sentencing calculation.

Thus, Mr. London's position is the starting point for the government's analysis should be much lower, presumably with downward revisions for the same reasons mentioned in the report.

The 9/23/13 response to the PSR closes with no recommendation for sentencing. It says a recommendation would follow later in a Sentencing Memorandum before sentencing. I think that is what was filed under seal on Monday.

I pondered again the US Attorney's filing from this week. A large portion of the comments are directed to countering the points made by Mr. London in his 9/23/13 filing. Many of the comments are specifically rebutted when you consider both documents side by side.

Many of the comments on page 15 through 25 of the government's filing on 4/7/14 are directed at the claim for probation. In particular the comments starting the bottom of page 23 are specifically directed to the need for jail time to communicate to the rest of society that even though insider trading is hard to find and harder to prove, when it is found and proved there will be jail time involved.

The argument would seem to be that as a society it is not good for us to say you can walk after committing intentional, clear, deliberate, profitable insider trading. In other words, a rapid confession doesn't keep you out of jail.

So there you have it. The AG is recommending 3 years. Mr. London is requesting probation.

Observations from a reader on
Scott London's family assets
4/9/14

A Mr. or Mrs. sjenson has been commenting on my blog to describe some family assets belonging to the London family that have apparently been moved into a Nevada corporation.

You can see the current discussion at an older post, *Sentencing recommendation and suggestion for lighter sentence for ex-KPMG partner's insider trading*. (http://goo.gl/yhnudx)

The commenter has several thoughts and questions.

The core of his/her idea seems to be wondering why assets would be moved into a Nevada corporation. If you have ever had contact with one of those outfits, you know they operate in a completely different world.

Check out the comments if you are interested.

His or her comments belong to him. Anyone have any thoughts or comments on the comments? All comments welcome. Of course, subject to maintaining a professional demeanor with the determination of what is professional being made by me!

London sentencing watch – request filed
to continue hearing three days, to April 24
4/15/14

On 4/14/14, the U.S. Attorney and Scott London's attorney filed a request to postpone the sentencing hearing for Mr. London from April 21 to April 24.

The reason cited is that Mr. London's attorney will be out of town on Monday. The filing says the court clerk indicated there is time available in the schedule on Thursday.

The court has not issued the order, but I would assume that it will easily be approved.

So we will wait patiently for a week from Thursday.

Insider trading sentencing watch – London's trading partner Shaw scheduled to be sentenced May 19
4/15/14

I've not been reading the federal court filings for Mr. Bryan Shaw, partner in crime of former KPMG partner Mr. Scott London. Started looking at them this evening.

Most pertinent information at the moment is that his sentencing hearing is scheduled for May 19, 2014 at 8 a.m.

The sentencing has been postponed several times.

After entering a guilty plea on May 20, 2013, the sentencing has been scheduled for:
- September 16
- November 18
- January 23
- February 24
- May 19

Sentencing position papers are due by May 5. The postponement to May 19 is the first one that orders sentencing papers to be filed. The docket does not indicate the U.S. probation staff have submitted a presentencing report (PSR).

Based on my limited knowledge, I'll guess that means the sentencing will be postponed again. I'll guess the PSR will probably be held until after Mr. London's sentencing and then the feds and Mr. Shaw's attorney will both need time to respond to the PSR.

London sentencing watch – scheduled for 4/24 at 11 am as of 4/21
4/21/14

The sentencing for Scott London on his guilty plea for insider trading has been moved back three hours. As of 4/21 he is still scheduled to be sentenced this Thursday, 4/24, but will be appearing at 11:00 a.m. Pacific time instead of 8:00 a.m.

I took a look at the docket this afternoon and found a few items that may be of wider interest.

Sentencing documents

Lots of documents have been filed under seal since my last post on sentencing. The government's sentencing memorandum was filed on 4/7; item #47 on the docket. I discussed the government's recommendation here and here.

On 4/10, there are three sealed documents. The first (#51) is a filing to request something be filed under seal. The next entry is an order granting the request. The following item (#53) is dated 4/1 but was entered 4/16 and is titled *"Defendants' Sentencing Memorandum, with Exhibits (attachments: Part 2, Part 3)."*

On 4/18, the government filed a notice it would make a filing under seal. The docket does not reflect that filing has yet been made.

On 4/21, Mr. London's attorney filed a notice to seal a document. The next entry, item #58, is titled *"Sealed Document – Defendant's Response to the Government's Sentencing Position."* That would be Mr. London's' reply to the government recommendation. The following entry orders that filing to be sealed. All three of those are dated 4/21 with a notation they were entered on 4/21.

Entry #59 is the judge's order, which says:

"IT IS HEREBY ORDERED THAT: Defendant's ex parte application for sealed filing is GRANTED. The document sought to be filed under seal, Defendant's Response to the Government's Sentencing Position, and the sealing application shall both be filed under seal and may not be thereafter viewed by any persons, other than the government and/or the U.S.P.O. without a request on showing of good cause."

Anyone have any idea why so many documents would be filed under seal at this point? Is something odd in the wind or is this the way cases go? Is there something of high visibility or particular sensitivity in the filings?

Update: 14 months.

Sentencing for Scott London still set for 11:00 a.m. today
4/24/14

As of 7:00 this morning, the federal PACER system still shows an order that sentencing will take place today, 4/24, at 11:00 Pacific time.

Mr. London pled guilty to one count of insider trading. The government's recommendation is three years. Mr. London's attorney has indicated he would recommend probation. No other filings visible since last update.

I'll update during the day as information becomes available. I have a lot of billable work to do, so won't be hanging out in downtown LA at the federal courthouse.

Update – 14 months.

14 months for Scott London in insider trading case
4/24/14

The *Los Angeles Times* is reporting *KPMG partner who gave tips to golf buddy sentenced for insider trading*. (http://goo.gl/nF3ZIb)

Stuart Pfeifer reports Judge George Wu sentenced Scott London to 14 months in federal prison and a $100,000 fine.

Defense counsel had argued for 6 to 12 months, according to the article.

More info to follow.

Update 1 at 12:35:

First 4 visible articles:

- 1st report 40 minutes ago *Los Angeles Times* – *KPMG partner who gave tips to golf buddy sentenced for insider trading*. (http://goo.gl/4k4dSc)
- 19 minutes ago – *Telegraph* – *Former KPMG partner Scott London jailed for 14 months for leading information*. (http://goo.gl/B5sPR4)
- 7 minutes ago - *Wall Street Journal* – *Former KPMG Partner Scott London Gets 14 Months in Prison for Insider Trading* (http://goo.gl/J5HJbj)
- 3 minutes ago - *Going Concern* – *Scott London Sentenced to 14 Months in the Can and a $100K Fine* (http://goo.gl/fuXZCQ)

The *Wall Street Journal* article says Mr. London will report to jail by July 18. Also gets three years probation after jail.

Update 2 – My understanding of the federal sentencing deal is you actually serve the time you are sentenced. However, there is an allowance for 54 days off the sentence for each year of good behavior. If my simple understanding is correct, that means time in jail would be 14 months minus 54 days, or about 1 year and 6 days.

Update 3 – Quotes from sentencing hearing today - *Other than that Mrs. Lincoln, how was the play?* (see next page)

Update 4: CNBC has video of Mr. London leaving court today. Nothing notable in the video or report other than the camera operator walking the camera forward into the side of Mr. London's head. Camera operator stepped around reporter and photographer for better shot and then stepped forward putting the lens into Mr. London's ear. Looks to me like fault goes to: camera operator. (http://goo.gl/wHqazR)

Update 5: There have been a couple dozen articles published in the last 4 hours. Seems like they are just rewriting the previous articles. Not much new info. One odd thing I need to go back and research is just what did Mr. London request for a sentence and what did his attorney request. Seems there have been several conflicting reports. As of quarter to 5, the sentencing documents are not visible on the PACER website.

I don't know the etiquette of the video part of the news biz, but I'm guessing that making contact on the subject of your camera work using the lens of your camera is not a particularly good career advancing move.

Update 6: *Judicial consequences and some major embarrassment consequences*. (http://goo.gl/GpLnd1)

Update 7: My perceptions on the *Sequence of arguments for sentencing in Scott London case* (see following page)

Update 8: *KPMG response to London sentencing* and my guess on next step for firm. (see following page)

Update 9, 4/25 1:45: I'm getting a huge amount of visitors to this page (well, huge for my little bitty site at least). So probably time for another disclosure. A long time ago I worked in the Albuquerque office of Peat Marwick Mitchell, as KPMG was known then. I enjoyed my time there and have the utmost respect for the colleagues that I worked with. I also am a practicing CPA providing audits to the nonprofit community. That makes me an infinitesimally small, sub-microscopic competitor to KPMG. Filter my comments as you wish.

Other than that Mrs. Lincoln, how was the play? – Quotes from Scott London sentencing hearing
4/24/14

A few quotes are filtering out in news reports about the sentencing today for Scott London over his admitted insider trading.

The Wall Street Journal provides the following quote in their article, *Former KPMG Partner Scott London Gets 14 Months in Prison for Insider Trading*: (http://goo.gl/mLqr6j)

"I deeply regret my actions," Mr. London is sited as telling the court. "I'm embarrassed and ashamed...I blame no one but myself."

And the line from a Bloomberg BusinessWeek article remind me of the old joke, "Other than that, how was the play Mrs. Lincoln?"

The readers over at *Going Concern* will light up over this one. From *Bloomberg's* *Ex-KPMG Auditor London Gets 14 Months in Insider-Trading Case*, the article quotes Mr. London that at his core he was an honest person. He then asked for community service and probation. (http://goo.gl/SyuNGN) (http://goo.gl/r1le9v)

From Stuart Pfeifer in the Los Angeles Times- *KPMG partner who gave tips to golf buddy sentenced for insider trading*. Mr. Pfeifer quotes Mr. London from an interview from a year ago with the Times saying he didn't know what he was thinking. He didn't know why there was a judgment lapse but there was one. Notice the passive voice. (http://goo.gl/p28bep)

Francine McKenna (@retheauditors) and Aaron Elstein (@InTheMkts) are tweeting about the use of passive voice in that comment.

Anyone know how to get the full text of a hearing in federal court? I know how to get rulings and filings through the PACER system, but not hearings. Any ideas?

Sequence of arguments for
sentencing in Scott London case
4/25/14

After the sentencing yesterday for former KPMG partner Scott London, I was confused by conflicting comments indicating the defense had both requested probation and a short jail sentence during the hearing. Those seem to be contradictory positions.

The *Wall Street Journal* article *Former KPMG Partner Scott London Gets 14 Months for Insider Trading* helps me put a few pieces together. (http://goo.gl/mLqr6j))

The article said the defense counsel, Mr. Braun initially suggested probation. The judge then indicated there would be jail time. Mr. Braun then suggested 6 to 12 months.

Putting together the pieces of information that are visible in print, here's what I think happened:

Federal guidelines point toward a sentence of 46 to 57 months. The U.S. Probation Office recommended a downward departure to 36 months. In the presentencing report the Assistant US Attorney agreed. I've mentioned that info before.

I think this was the sequence yesterday:

The prosecutor asked for 36 months in court.

The defense requested probation. I'm not sure if it was just Mr. London's attorney making that request or whether he and his attorney made that plea.

The judge made a comment that prison time was necessary both because of the seriousness of the crime and to be a deterrent for others.

With probation off the table, Mr. London's attorney asked for 6 to 12 months.

The judge issued sentence of 14 months with 3 years probation after jail.

More context on the sentencing hearing for Scott London.
Why I am writing so much about this case.
6/3/14

Found some more comments from coverage of the sentencing for Scott London that changes the perception of the hearing. At least it changes my perception. Mentioned this in the previous few posts. Wish I had been in the sentencing hearing.

Look at the comments I mentioned earlier:

The *Wall Street Journal* – *Former KPMG Partner Scott London Gets 14 Months in Prison for Insider Trading*: He regrets his actions. He is ashamed, embarrassed. He blames only himself. (http://goo.gl/mLqr6j)

Bloomberg BusinessWeek – *Ex-KPMG Auditor London Gets 14 Months in Insider-Trading Case*: He is an honest person at his core. He requested community service and probation. (http://goo.gl/tTy9MZ)

Stuart Pfeifer -*Los Angeles Times*- *KPMG partner who gave tips to golf buddy sentenced for insider trading*. Mr. Pfeifer provide a quote from Mr. London provided during an interview a year earlier using passive voice saying there was a judgment lapse. (http://goo.gl/JXcXp0)

I sense a perspective of "I'm a good guy" in that quote at BusinessWeek. That one sentence suggests a lack of ownership in the fiasco. It is at its core a rationalization. On the other hand, the quote provided by the WSJ indicates ownership of the situation.

The year earlier comment got attention in the twitter world for the passive voice. That phrasing suggests the mess just sort of happened. Remember that was a year ago, in the midst of the massive reporting taking place then. Long before sentencing and possibly in the midst of various negotiations.

All of those are bits and pieces of the story.

More context

Now the point: add to all of that the following comments. Consider whether it changes your perspective.

The article from Mr. Pfeifer above has a time stamp of 11:50 a.m. on 4/24/14. The same article was updated that afternoon with a 5:44 p.m. timestamp as *Former KPMG partner sentenced for insider trading*.

(http://goo.gl/mzdmNW)

Check out this comment which was in the 5:44 article but not in the 11:50 article. The sequence of comments was I'm embarrassed, I'm ashamed, I disappointed everybody especial those close, I disappointed myself.

He wiped tears away as he sat down.

The earlier article had no quotes from the hearing, only the comment from a year ago. That quote from the hearing in the later article provides a different perspective. The comments in court show ownership and taking responsibility.

On the other hand, every one of those comments was in front of a judge and had the obvious goal of trying to minimize the jail sentence. On the other, other hand, CPAs are not usually very good actors.

Let me reorganize the above comments to see what picture it shows. I will only quote those words directly attributed to Mr. London.

The comment from a year ago:

"I have no idea what I was thinking," … "I don't know why there was a lapse of judgment but there was."

Fast forward a year, past the plea deal, prep for sentencing, and now appearing for sentence. It has been a year, which could allow some time for coming to terms with the underlying causes. Here are several comments during the hearing, with my wild guess on the sequence:

"I'm at the core an honest person," …

"I deeply regret my actions," … "I'm embarrassed and ashamed…

I'm embarrassed and ashamed," *(overlap with previous quote)* … "I disappointed everyone close to me. Most of all, I disappointed myself."

"… I blame no one but myself."

Looking at only those fragments of comments from longer comments shows progress on taking ownership.

Why the odd pose in that photo?

Check out the photo of Mr. London in that *LA Times* article. Looks odd.

He is leaning to his right, has his right arm up in a defensive position, looks a bit distressed, and is covering his left ear with his left hand.

Why would he be in such an odd position? Is he mad at the photographer? Getting ready for an exchange of blows?

Put together what happened a few seconds earlier and a different picture appears (sorry for the pun).

Just a moment before that snapshot, a CNBC camera operator had pushed a camera lens into Mr. London's ear. He had been struck by a camera. Looks to me like the camera operator stepped into Mr. London. (I hope it is a career limiting move at CNBC to commit battery on the subject of one's camera work. From my outside perspective, that seems to be exquisitely unprofessional.) You can see the clip here which I mentioned here in update 4.

That odd pose makes sense. The I'm-still-learning-about-this-journalism-stuff part of me wonders why that is the snapshot used to illustrate the story when the photog probably took a hundred pictures of Mr. London walking from the courthouse to his car.

Why do I share this information?

This is rather minor trivia in a story that is now old news. So why this post?

There are several reasons.

By diving deep into a story, I am learning and growing more than with just one or two posts.

By putting my thoughts into writing, I am learning to articulate my observations. Hopefully I'm learning how to tell a complex story. Essentially, I'm doing it for myself – even if nobody ever reads this post, I benefit. Seth Godin and Tom Peters explain this idea. ()

Also, someday I'd like to write a book about this situation.

(**Update** during editing: The book I pondered is now in your hands! Or in pixels on your screen.)

Finally, it is possible (not likely, but possible) that some people following my discussion of the KPMG fiasco might be interested in the subtle details.

KPMG response to Scott London sentencing; possible next step for firm
4/25/14

KPMG provided me the following statement regarding the sentencing yesterday of Scott London:

> "It was appropriate that Scott London was held accountable today for the consequences of his illegal and unethical actions."

An extremely vague, hard to understand comment in the CNBC report yesterday, yes, the one wherein the camera operator ran the camera lens into the side of Mr. London's face, indicated KPMG had taken some financial action against Mr. London. The article cited Mr. London's attorney as saying that matter had been resolved through the partnership agreement. I don't understand what that means, but my wild guess is the partnership agreement allowed closing out his retirement account or possibly putting that on hold for the moment. I'll make another wild guess that he wasn't allowed to pull any money out of his retirement account.

My businessman's understanding of the law suggests the guilty plea followed by sentencing would clear the deck to let KPMG proceed with litigation against Mr. London to recover their costs. My wild guess is that KPMG quickly reimbursed Herbalife for the cost of reauditing the Herbalife financial statements for three years. My further guess is that KPMG will be looking to Mr. London for reimbursement, likely through litigation.

The story isn't over. I'll keep you updated over the next many months.

Note during editing: Posted my follow-up to that idea about two months later. That discussion is pulled into this point in the book.

Why KPMG won't be suing Scott London
6/19/14

After the sentencing of Scott London to 14 months in prison, KPMG issued me (and the rest of the world) a statement saying:

> "It was appropriate that Scott London was held accountable for the consequence of his illegal and unethical action."

As I mentioned earlier, there were some comments in public by Mr. London's attorney that KPMG and Mr. London had worked out something through the partnership agreement. My guess is they closed out his capital account.

My guess at the time was that the sentencing cleared the path for KPMG to sue Mr. London. They would definitely have cause since the Herbalife reaudit cost around $15M, and they probably sent the bill to KPMG, who probably paid it quickly. I'll guess that KPMG paid for the reaudit of the other two clients. (http://goo.gl/wle1ay)

So, will KPMG sue Mr. London?

When I tweeted about my post, Francine McKenna followed up with a tweet saying something to the effect that this was the end of the case. Nothing else would be heard.

I recently visited with Ms. McKenna. She explained why she didn't think there would be any lawsuit. She gave me permission to share her reasons.

She thinks KPMG will not pursue any litigation against Mr. London because they don't want any more publicity. The criminal case is settled. Mr. London will be reporting to prison next month. The visibility of the case has dropped off the radar screen. Other than this teeny tiny blog and an upcoming CPE session next Wednesday, 6/25 – lots more about that soon.

So, the first major reason for no suit – *avoid creating more publicity.*

The very visible criminal prosecution and investigation by the feds and KPMG has shown clearly there weren't any other staff involved. A boundary has been set around the number of companies involved.

There is a clear separation between KPMG and Mr. London's actions.

The Thomas Flanagan case with Deloitte is quite different. Mr. Flanagan was a vice chairman of Deloitte LLP who was sentenced to prison for 21 months for insider trading. Ms. McKenna described to me in that situation, Deloitte had to sue Mr. Flanagan to show there was separation between him and the firm. In the London & KPMG situation, the feds had already researched the issue, put a boundary around the persons involved and companies traded, and resolved the case. All that happened before KPMG knew there was an issue. Thus, KPMG doesn't need to establish distance. ()

Unlike Mr. London who passed tips to his golf buddy, Mr. Flanagan personally traded on the inside information.

Here is some additional info on Mr. Flanagan's incarceration:

He was sentenced to 21 months in federal prison, as reported by Bloomberg on 10/26/12. He was also given one year supervised release and a $100,000 fine. A reporting date 60 days after sentencing would give an estimated incarceration date of about 12/26/12. (http://goo.gl/YZGWRM)

The Bureau of Prisons' inmate locator service shows Thomas P Flanagan (Register Number: 44822-424, age 66) has a release date of 7/23/14. That release date would be about 64 days short of 21 months after the estimated reporting date. That would in turn be consistent with the 53 days credit for good time that I've read is available for each year in federal prison. (http://goo.gl/nlBpHZ or www.bop.gov/inmateloc/)

The BOP site says his location is the <u>Chicago Residential Reentry Management</u> facility. That means he is out of federal prison. He is either home under supervision by the Chicago RRM or he is residing at the Chicago RRM facility. (http://goo.gl/BUBSC0)

Back to KPMG and Mr. London...

So, the second reason we won't see any litigation - *KPMG is disassociated from the inside trading mess.*

Finally, it is possible there could be something else involved. Ms. McKenna doesn't know what it could be, but there is a possibility there might be something else.

Perhaps another client. Perhaps a different staff person doing something on the periphery. Perhaps something unrelated that's embarrassing to the firm but might surface during trial.

Perhaps KPMG just doesn't want to risk arousing any sleeping dogs that nobody knows are still sleeping.

So, the third reason for no litigation – *keep unknown issues unknown.*

I will add another reason – it's probably not worth the effort financially.

How much could KPMG recover? They already grabbed whatever is in the retirement/capital account, which I will guess is several million and is probably the bulk of any Big 4 partner's net worth. How much more could there be? A commenter on my blog points to a vineyard that is owned by Mr. London's wife. As a wild guess, there could be a couple of houses for investment purposes. What could that all add up to? A million? 3? 5?

There is the issue of an unknown amount of legal fees for the initial investigation, negotiations with 3 audit clients, and negotiations with Mr. London regarding his capital account. Those would be premium fees since the big firms draw on the best law firms who charge proportionate fees. Any guesses on how much that might be? Quarter of a million? Half? Full million?

Oh, and filing a lawsuit would require having all the documents, exhibits, and filings ready to go before giving anything to the clerk of the court. How much would that be? Another hundred grand? Quarter million?

Here's the string of my guesses on the overall financial picture: KPMG is out $15M spent on reimbursing Herbalife, plus several more million on the other two reaudits, plus the unknown amount of legal fees already incurred, plus legal fees to file a suit, less a million or two or three reimbursement from the retirement/capital account, which leaves the firm out something in the range of $12M to $18M. My wild guess of a potential recovery is maybe $1M to $4M. Taking the low/high and high/low of those wild guesses gives a possible net loss position after litigation recovery of something in the range of $8M to $17M. There is still a substantial loss even with successful litigation recovery.

My guess? The potential recovery of a few million is a huge number to you and me, but in the overall scheme of a Big 4 firm, that is probably in the range of write-off authority for a regional partner. Might be worth giving up on a recovery just to never again see this case mentioned in the Wall Street Journal. Might be worth it so no internal KPMG staff or partners ever have to deal with it again.

The firm will let it go. The potential payoff isn't significant. That amount, whatever it might be, is more than offset by the known risk of new publicity and unknown risk of sleeping dogs racing around the courtroom.

The fourth reason for no litigation – *not worth it financially*.

Full disclosure: A long time ago I worked at Peat, Marwick, Mitchell for three years in their Albuquerque office. PMM was the predecessor to KPMG. I am a sole practitioner providing audits and reviews to the nonprofit community. Filter my comments as you wish.

Please remember that links to articles on the internet have a short URL at the end of the paragraph linking to the article. For example:

(http://goo.gl/yjh2rb)

In addition, live links are available at the publisher's web site. You can find the live links at:

http://riverstonefinancepress.com/tragedy-links/

Shaw sentencing

Sentencing date postponed for inside trader Bryan Shaw; Feds request 6 months

5/24/14

On May 5, the presiding judge postponed sentencing from May 19 to June 2 for Bryan Shaw, who pled guilty to insider trading. He based his trades on information provided by Scott London, formerly regional audit PIC for KPMG.

The U.S. Attorney is requesting 6 months in jail, 3 years supervised released, and a $3,000 fine.

Sentencing level under federal guidelines would be 37 to 46 months. Because of the extensive assistance in building the case against Mr. London, the U.S. Attorney calculates the guidelines would indicate a sentence of 12 to 18 months. Because of aggravating and mitigating factors, the prosecutors recommend a below-guideline sentence of 6 months.

In addition, the government requests three years of supervised release. Prosecutor also request a fine of $3,000, acknowledging Mr. Shaw has already paid about $1.9 million to the SEC as a fine ($658,000) and disgorgement of profits ($1,271,787). Sentencing guidelines suggest a fine in the range of $3k to $30k, so the recommended fine is at the bottom of the range.

The report indicates the initial analysis of insider trading gains were $1,270,000 which was increased by subsequent SEC analysis to about $1,600,000 of gain.

The defense sentencing recommendation is probation, with home confinement if the judge considers it necessary.

This position is based on many cited factors, but particularly the extensive cooperation provided by Mr. Shaw. The filing says that Mr. Shaw went to the FBI and U.S. Attorney before they knew of the SEC's interest in Mr. Shaw and before the FBI or US Attorney had any idea there was an insider case or any involvement from Mr. London. This cooperation allowed the government to build a case in three months in contrast to the typical year needed to build an insider trading case.

In addition, Mr. Shaw's attorney points out that the information and cooperation provided made such a strong case that it was likely Mr. London would immediately confess.

The filing also points out the huge deterrent effect of the massive publicity of getting that now famous photo of handing over the $5,000 cash. If you recall, that pic was in most newspapers across the country, including first page, above-the-fold position in the *Wall Street Journal*. (http://goo.gl/6i7JDR)

Stay tuned. Sentencing on June 2.

Bryan Shaw sentencing watch. – Update on chronology.
6/1/14

The federal PACER system does not show any updates as of the evening of 6/1 that would change the scheduled sentencing of Bryan Shaw on 6/2 for conspiracy for his insider trading based on information provided by former KPMG partner Scott London. Scheduled for 8:00 a.m. on June 2.

The defense has filed a supplemental sentencing document that spells out in more detail the cooperation provided by Mr. Shaw. I read through it and glanced at the initial complaint against Mr. London. Here are a few highlights:

February 8, 2013 – Mr. Shaw rolled over on Mr. London and rolled hard.

He met with the US attorney, two SEC attorneys, and FBI agent before DOJ, FBI, and SEC knew the scheme existed. From the filing:

"Mr. Shaw meets at the U.S. Attorney's Office with Assistant U.S. Attorney James Bowman, an FBI Special Agent, and two SEC attorneys. He provides a full confession of his conduct and detailed information about London's involvement and about the specific companies and trades affected by insider information. (Complaint ¶ 22). Prior to Mr. Shaw providing this information, the DOJ and FBI had no knowledge that the insider trading scheme existed, and the SEC had only issued an initial subpoena to Mr. Shaw in connection with its administrative examination."

Mr. Shaw initiated two in-person meetings and multiple phone calls to Mr. London. During those discussions Mr. London volunteered inside information on the following dates:

- February 14
- February 19
- February 20 – contains an odd comment which I'm quoting: "London again references rumors about Herbalife going private, stating that "we're gonna make money" when that happens. London laughs when Mr. Shaw responds, "I know that – why do you think I'm paying you?" (Complaint ¶ 27)."
- February 21
- February 21 – in person meeting with transfer of $5K; additional inside information passed
- February 26

- February 27
- February 28
- March 4
- March 7 – in person meeting with transfer of $5K; photo from the surveillance hit all the papers; additional inside information passed

Now let's go back to the criminal complaint dated April 11, 2013.

- March 20 – FBI confronts Mr. London at his residence in the morning.
- April 3 – interview with Mr. London at the U.S. Attorney's office with two FBI agents, federal prosecutor, and two SEC attorneys, with interview initially given under limited use immunity.
- April 9 – I think this is when the news broke.

Some stray thoughts:

The scheme appears to have been dormant until 2/14/13, although I need to backtrack the activity some more to be sure. Not sure when it went dormant.

The amount of cash is generally referred to as $60,000 or more. Of this, $10,000 was provided at the direction of the FBI. Add in $12K for a watch gives around $72K, less $10k provided by the FBI means $62k was volunteered by Mr. Shaw. Setting aside the concert tickets and dinners, that is the amount Mr. Shaw volunteered as Mr. London's share.

I recall a comment that I won't look up at the moment that Mr. London indicated (I think it was him saying that was the understanding but need to double-check that) that the proceeds would be split in thirds: one share to Mr. Shaw, one to Mr. London, and one for taxes.

If you go with the trading proceeds in the various federal filings of about $1.27M, then the one-third split would have been $423K. If you go with the $1,600K amount the federal sentencing recommendation says the SEC says they subsequently calculated, then the one-third split would be $533K.

That means Mr. Shaw shorted Mr. London either $361K or $471K.

If you are really so interested that you read to the end of this post, then you will really, really want to watch the news wires tomorrow. (Did I just say wires? Um. Yeah. Make that watch your twitter feed.)

Bryan Shaw sentenced for conspiracy re: insider trading case with former KPMG partner Scott London
6/2/14

Initial report at about 12:25 from CNBC: 5 months in prison. (http://goo.gl/ubX090)

Will update during day as more reports become visible.

Updates:

Reuters reports *Jeweler who traded on ex-KPMG partner's tips sentenced to prison*. Report says five months in prison. No fine, in light of $1.9M already paid to SEC as penalty and disgorgement. Prosecution was only asking for $3K fine; that is a minor difference between $0 and $3K. (http://goo.gl/lFhhcm)

Los Angeles Times runs that infamous parking lot photo at top of article: *Informant in KPMG insider trading case sentenced to 5 months in prison*. The reporter, Riley Snyder, was obviously in court during sentencing provided some of the context you won't otherwise see in reporting or transcripts. He had several family members with him in court. He handed a handwritten apology to the judge. (http://goo.gl/xq0VfX)

With a shaky voice he promised the judge would never see him again.

Post-Periodical – *Encino Jeweler Sentenced for Insider Trading* – Also, 3 years supervised release. (http://goo.gl/rT2Y7O)

5:30 update – From the few stats available on my site, it looks like there are quite a few people clicking through to the articles linked above. Good. I'll provide a few more:

LA Business Journal – *Insider Trading Co-Conspirator Sentenced* - Extremely short summary – 12 lines. (http://goo.gl/QxA5Ay)

6/3 update:

LA Times article by Riley Snyder updated at 7:01 p.m. – *Bryan Shaw sentenced to prison in KPMG insider trading case*. A few new details. The judge recommends a federal facility for nonviolent offenders, either in Lompoc or Taft. Upland's ex-mayor, John Pomierski, served his time in Taft. Mr. Shaw has 60 days to report, which would be about 8/2.

(http://goo.gl/I1tXM4)

Minor details of Bryan Shaw's
sentencing for insider trading case
6/17/14

The sentencing documents are available on the federal PACER system for Bryan Shaw's conspiracy conviction. Not really any new information. Did want to mention what is listed there. Also want to mention tracking info in the Bureau of Prison's system for both Mr. Shaw and Mr. London.

As mentioned previously, the judge sentenced Mr. Shaw to 5 months in prison.

Other terms include 3 years supervised release. As a general concept, if a person violates any of the terms of supervised release, the person could go back to federal prison for some or all of the time subject to supervised release.

No fine, but there is a special assessment of $100.

He must report to the Bureau of Prisons by noon on August 1, 2014. That would be 60 days from sentencing and just over 6 weeks from now.

The court suggested confinement at either Lompoc or Taft, California.

Just checked the sentencing document for Mr. London. The judge made a very general recommendation of a facility in Southern California.

Mr. London is listed in the Bureau of Prisons' *inmate database*. His status is "not in BOP custody". Mr. Shaw is not yet listed in the BOP database. (http://goo.gl/nlBpHZ)

Reporting to jail

Scott London expected to report to prison on Friday; Bryan Shaw is already in custody.
7/18/14

At sentencing, Judge Wu ordered Scott London to report to prison by noon on July 18. That is today.

When I checked the Federal Bureau of Prisons Inmate Locator Service on Thursday evening, it showed Mr. London's status as not in custody with no release date. That's what I expected.

(http://goo.gl/nlBpHZ)

Then I checked on Mr. Shaw. The court sentenced Mr. Shaw to 5 months with recommendation of confinement at either Taft or Lompoc with orders to report by August 1, 2014.

He is already in custody.

There are two listings for Bryan Shaw in the BOP Inmate Locator. I looked at the data for Bryan Shaw, register number 64829-112, age 53, white male. He is in custody at Taft CI with release date of 11/28/14.

That is not what I expected. How odd.

The reporting date was ordered by the judge to be August 1. With a 5 month sentence, that would give an expected release date of January 1, 2015. A release date of 11/28 would imply a reporting date of 6/28, not 8/1.

Went to the federal PACER system and sorted out my confusion. On June 27, Judge Wu granted a request to advance the surrender date to June 30.

On July 16, there is a notation in his docket the court clerk verified that as of that date he was in custody.

So, my read of the situation is Mr. Shaw reported early on 6/28 and has an expected release date of 11/28.

Will post an update when Mr. London is reported in custody.

Scott London is in prison on 7/19/14. Expected release date 7/23/15.
7/19/14

Looks like he surrendered into custody yesterday.

The Bureau of Prisons has an Inmate Locator Service which provides location and incarceration data for all federal prisoners since 1982. Lookup is by name or register number.

As of Saturday morning, 7/19, the locator shows Scott London (register 64641-112) is incarcerated at Taft Correctional Institute, near Bakersfield, California.

His posted release date is 7/23/15.

His sentence was 14 months, which with an ordered report date of 7/18/14 would mean the expected release date would be 9/14/15.

I've read that in the federal system, there is a 53 day credit per year of the sentence for each year. That is why sometimes a federal sentence is one year and one day. That gives the defendant a 53 day credit which can be lost by bad behavior, which in turn creates high motivation for playing nice.

A release date of 7/23/15 would be 57 days earlier than the expected date. Thus, this indicates the credit is around 57 days.

Mentioned yesterday that Bryan Shaw reported early and that he is at Taft CI. I double checked this morning and he is still listed at Taft. It's confusing to me that the BoP would assign co-conspirators to the same facility, especially since one rolled over on the other.

Why am I focusing on Mr. Shaw's and Mr. London's arrival in prison and the time they will be there?

To emphasize the hard-earned wages of fraud.

Mr. London commented several times in his June 26 interview that he did not ponder the consequences of his insider trading. Well, for everyone else, these blog posts provide a picture of what consequences are earned by breaking the law.

Scott London is now in Lompoc penitentiary.
8/28/14

As part of the final editing of my book, I checked the locations of Mr. London and Mr. Shaw in the federal prison system. You can look up such things at the Bureau of Prisons Inmate Locator.

Mr. Shaw is still at Taft Correctional Institute. Last time I looked, they were both at Taft.

Mr. London has been moved up the coast to USP Lompoc (United States Penitentiary). That is a medium security prison with an attached minimum security facility. The facility is a mile or less from Lompoc, maybe 2 miles from the ocean, and is immediately adjacent to Vandenberg Air Force Base.

Mr. London's official release date is still July 23, 2015. Mr. Shaw is still scheduled for release November 28, 2014, the day after Thanksgiving.

Public interviews

CPE event of the year – 4 hour ethics class featuring interview with Scott London
6/20/14

Well, at least I think it will be the event to see. Next Wednesday, June 25, Scott London will be interviewed in a webcast presented by The Pros and The Cons. (http://goo.gl/ZOJqVO or www.theprosandthecons.com)

To my recollection, all the previous interviews of Mr. London were brief events entering or leaving a court room. There have been a few conversations with reporters, but nothing in detail. This will be the first, in-depth interview I know of. Several hours will allow the time to give full, nuanced answers and explore follow-up questions.

Class brochure here. (http://goo.gl/yzpfhK)

I'll be tuning in and scribbling notes furiously so I can flesh out more of my reporting on Mr. London.

2 interviews with Scott London
6/21/14

Two interviews of Scott London have appeared quite recently in advance of his marathon interview in a CPE class:

- **6/21 – Quentin Fottrell at Market Watch** – Confessions of an insider trader on the eve of his prison sentence.
  (http://goo.gl/xZ0OTI)
- **6/16 – Walter Pavlo at Forbes** – Fmr KPMG Partner Scott London Shares Cautionary Tale Before Prison
  (http://goo.gl/7m0e64)

A few ideas from each of the interviews and a few of my observations.

Quentin Fottrell at Market Watch –

Mr. London perceives that insider trading is rampant.

He asserts he received about $50,000 in total, which *includes* the Rolex (which he rarely wore), and concert tickets.

He says he was helping out a friend by sharing information. It wasn't until much later that he realized he was way over the line. Several comments in the interview suggest a long, slow, slippery slope.

Reminds me of the story of a frog in a kettle. To boil a frog to death, put it in a pot of cold water, then turn up the heat. The slow change in temperature will not alert the frog and it will stay in the water until it dies.

Mr. London told the interviewer his salary was closer to $650,000 and not the $900,000 mentioned in court filings.

If he had known beforehand the impact on his family and friends, he would not have shared the information. That comment is hindsight now, but I think that's probably correct.

If a fraudster could foresee the look of fright and shock on the faces of the spouse and children, I think it would scare off a lot of would-be fraudsters.

At one point in my career, I was in the room during an interview with a fraudster. The person's spouse was also in the room. I wish, oh I wish, I could have taken a picture of the spouse's face during the discussion. That look would freeze anyone in their tracks.

Mr. London has not seen or talked to Mr. Shaw since the first interview with the FBI. After that interview he did realize Mr. Shaw had been making excuses to avoid socializing.

He has seen a therapist four or five times for two hours each session. That is a very good thing for him and for his health.

Mr. London shares that he was under some major pressure in his position and was working rather brutal hours with lots of travel. He had been asking to move out of that position for three years.

He says he's being paid for the upcoming interview, a couple hundred bucks an hour for somewhere around 10 or 15 hours.

He indicated he's hoping for a significant reduction from the 14 month sentence. This is a reasonable expectation.

I have learned there is something in the range of a 53 day credit for good behavior for each year in federal prison. From looking at two situations (John Pomierski, former mayor of the city of Upland and Thomas Flanagan, former vice chair of Deloitte), I've learned there are additional credits. In addition to the approximately 53 day credit, both of those men spent the last few months of a federal sentence in a halfway house.

So, 53 days off a 14 month sentence would be just over 12 months. Knock one or three months off the end of that, for reasons I don't quite understand, means the time in federal prison could be somewhere between nine and 12 months.

Mr. Fottrell commented that Mr. London has been very open and candid in the interview. Not quite what he had been expecting. The interview communicates an attitude of optimism, repentance, and ownership of his behavior.

Check out the interview for yourself.

Walter Pavlo at Forbes

Mr. Pavlo's interview with Mr. London is much shorter.

After reading the interview in Market Watch, a few comments in this interview fall into place.

He is not able to identify the reasons he violated his own moral and ethical codes, but guesses it comes down to other things going on in his life. Two specific factors he mentions are being in the same position for a long time, possibly too long, and wanting to help a friend in distress.

Reasons for speaking out now are to prevent others from getting into the same trouble. He hopes to highlight the collateral damage.

The personal consequences of the situation have been severe. He says dealing with the surge of media attention and overall embarrassment has been the toughest battle of his life.

Worse than that is the harm to others, specifically his family, friends, and KPMG.

Loss of friends and colleagues from work in the same company for 30 years has been very difficult. From previous published articles and court filings, we know that all staff at KPMG have been told to have absolutely no contact with Mr. London.

You can check out an upcoming 4 hour interview with Mr. London and pick up CPE hours at the same time. (http://goo.gl/euQETY)

Interview with Scott London during CPE webcast
6/26/14

Scott London was interviewed at length during a CPE webcast presented June 25, 2014. The class was presented by Gary Zuene, of The Pros and Cons.

Mr. London was remarkably open.

He repeatedly accepted full blame for the insider trading. At several points he explained the context, pressures he was under, and actions by others (especially his golfing buddy) that help us understand the situation better. Each time he mentioned something outside of himself he again said that he is responsible. He is to blame.

At one point he made a comment for which an inference could be made that his golfing buddy might have responsibly for the insider trading. He quickly added that it is his fault.

Michael Rapoport has an article in the Wall Street Journal on the interview: *Prison-Bound KPMG Ex-Partner Remorseful for Insider Tips*. Remorseful is a good description. It's a good article. Check it out. (http://goo.gl/wdFNcQ)

Nervous? Understandably so.

It seemed like Mr. London was nervous and uncomfortable during the interview. Imagine that!

He was exposing himself to scrutiny by everyone, including people who will be quite critical. He was sharing some of his psychological imperfections. He hinted at some personality flaws he is now trying to explore. I picked up on some he was suggesting. A psychologist could watch the interview and discern several unflattering parts of his personality that he unintentionally revealed.

Oh, and he's also going to prison within a month.

No wonder he was nervous and uncomfortable. There were only 2 breaks of 10 minutes each. The technology used by CPA Crossings put all of the interviewers on screen the entire time. It would be a rare person that would go on camera for four hours in such a situation. Even rarer would be a person who would appear as composed as any of the interviewers. I'd be very worried about someone who could be calm, cool, and collected in such a situation.

Mr. Zuene thanked Mr. London at the end of the interview for being so open and sharing so deeply.

(**Update during editing**: Anyone reading this book want to subject themselves a 4 hour live interview when you were caught doing something dumb? Count me out.)

This is the first in a series of blog posts I will write about the interview. There are a lot of comments in the interview that we can all learn from.

Mr. London said he routinely encounters the attitude that CPAs have to take an ethics class. I have heard those comments. Sort of the way you refer to getting some cavities filled or putting new tires on the car.

That is an understandable reaction as I ponder a lot of the ethics classes I've attended over the years. Checking off that state board requirement is just a part of the dreariness of meeting minimum requirements.

One of the changes Mr. London suggested we as a profession need to make is for ethics classes to be interesting. We need to figure out a way to make those classes appealing.

This class makes that change. It is a wide-ranging conversation. A great mixture of details on this fiasco, ethics in general, cases addressed at the state board level, and how the situation intersects with other accounting and auditing issues. It briefly brings in bigger issues in the economy.

Comments from Scott London during interview – part 1
7/7/14

On June 26, 2014, Scott London was interviewed in a four-hour CPE webcast on professional ethics.

The course was presented by The Pros and The Cons, which is run by Gary Zuene, CPA.

(http://goo.gl/ZOJqVO or www.theprosandthecons.com)

There are two published interviews that took place before the CPE session:

• 6/21 – Quentin Fottrell at *Market Watch* – *Confessions of an insider trader on the eve of his prison sentence* (http://goo.gl/xZ0OTI)

• 6/16 – Walter Pavlo at *Forbes* – *Fmr KPMG Partner Scott London Shares Cautionary Tale Before Prison.* (http://goo.gl/7m0e64)

I've seen two articles discussing the interview:

• 6/25 – Michael Rapoport at *Wall Street Journal* - *Prison-Bound KPMG Ex-Partner Remorseful for Insider Tips.* (http://goo.gl/wdFNcQ)

• 6/27 – Michael Cohn at *Accounting Today* – Former *KPMG Partner Scott London Speaks out Before Starting Prison Term.* (http://goo.gl/CrrUs7)

This post will summarize some of the comments from that interview that I found to be of particular interest.

The goal of this series of posts is to get the interview comments organizing into related topics.

Context for this series

I am presenting my comments about the interview with only a few narrative statements. At some later point I will correlate this with other news reports.

I won't comment now about my perceptions or how we interpret Mr. London's comments. That is for another series of posts. Maybe.

How did the insider trading scheme develop?

Mr. London indicated he met Bryan Shaw in the early 2000s. They became friends. Other news reports indicate they were golfing buddies. Their wives were friends, not particularly close Mr. London said, but still they were friends.

Perhaps you recall a discussion in the Going Concern blog about exchanges on Facebook between the Shaws and Londons. They were the typical banter that happens amongst social friends.

(http://goo.gl/uY7dVq)

Mr. London indicated his buddy Bryan Shaw is an active investor. Mr. Shaw did a lot of research and presumably had a lot of trading in his accounts.

In somewhere around 2008 Mr. Shaw started asking Mr. London the kinds of questions that a friend would ask.

I would imagine these would be things like *what has you so tied up that we had to cancel our tee time? Or what's got you so stressed this week?* Something that would obviously be a problem in hindsight could be something like *so what did Herbalife do* **this** *time that has you working so many hours* **again***?*

Questions like that would have been relatively innocuous at the time.

Mr. London wonders today whether he was being groomed at that point.

Mr. London insists there was not any nonpublic information passed before about 2010. Mr. Shaw was attentive to the names of clients who were generating overtime for Mr. London. He was likely making inferences and in fact was trading on it.

In around 2010, Mr. Shaw told Mr. London what he was doing – making trades based on inferences from their casual conversations. Mr. London says he was surprised by it.

That's where the slippery slope came in. Mr. London started giving a bit more information in response to slightly more detailed questions.

In late 2010, Mr. London became aware that Mr. Shaw's business was struggling. That's when he crossed the line and started sharing some nonpublic information.

It started relatively low-key and innocent but then shifted to something far more serious.

Mr. London said that if he had been asked something like hey I've got this great scheme to make us a bunch of money, Mr. London is confident he would've said forget it.

Next post: The payoffs and a quiet time.

Comments from Scott London interview – part 2
7/9/14

This is the second in a series of posts describing comments in an interview of Scott London during a four-hour CPE session on June 26. The course was presented by The Pros and The Cons.

(http://goo.gl/ZOJqVO or www.theprosandthecons.com)

The payoffs

Mr. London says he got around $50,000 in total. He thinks that Mr. Shaw exaggerated the jewelry and concert tickets in order to make the playoffs look bigger. He thinks Mr. Shaw may have paid $3,000 for the watch.

The ticket arrangement is what you might expect amongst friends. Mr. London said that sometimes Mr. Shaw would get the tickets for the two couples evening out and then Mr. London would pick up the dinner. Sometimes it would be the other way around.

Mr. Shaw gets lots of jewelry from customers as trade-ins. Sometimes Mr. London would buy some of those jewelry items from Mr. Shaw and some of them were gifts.

The currency payments started off small at $1,000 or $3,000. The largest at one time was $10,000. As Mr. London thinks of it now, it seems like it was random.

If those recollections are correct, the amount involved is less than the commonly reported $70,000.

A quiet time

When Bryan Shaw's account at Fidelity was closed, the passing of information stopped.

Mr. London said he knew it was stupid and it probably could become an issue in the future. He realized they shouldn't have been passing information and trading on it.

I don't have a transcript of the CPE session so can't look up the exact words, so those comments may have just been what he was thinking at the time. If I caught the phrasing right, I think there was an actual conversation between them that this was a dumb idea.

From the spring of 2012 until early 2013 there was no activity.

No passing of information. No insider trading.

Comments from Scott London interview – part 3
7/11/14

This is the third in a series of posts describing comments in an interview of Scott London during a four-hour CPE session on June 26.

Status with Bureau of Prisons

As an aside, the Bureau of Prisons has an Inmate Locator Service, which provides public disclosure of federal inmates.

On July 10, Scott London is listed in their database. His register number is 64641-112.

His status is *Not in BOP Custody* with a release date of Unknown.

The sting

Let's step outside the interview. At a time I'll tie in later, the SEC called Mr. Shaw. He poured out the whole story.

Then the FBI got involved and the sting started.

Back to the interview.

In early 2013 Mr. London received three or four phone calls from Mr. Shaw asking for more information.

On the surface, he was trying to start the insider trading again. At a deeper level, this obviously would have been part of the sting. Obviously, those calls would have all been recorded.

Mr. London said no each of the first several times.

Eventually he agreed and started passing nonpublic information again. That is the information we can read about in the criminal information and statement of facts.

Later I'll cross link the dates.

The sting resulted in a confrontation, confession, criminal charges, and photo splashed on the front page of the Wall Street Journal.

Was the sting necessary?

Mr. London disagreed with a comment that the feds had to set up the sting in order to charge him. He indicated that he would have confessed immediately when confronted. That is likely true. However, no federal agents knew that.

Let's ponder what the feds had before the sting.

Mr. Shaw's apparently an active trader. Activity in his accounts would indicate that a small handful of his presumably large number of trades were home runs. They happen to correspond to major public information being released, but that could just be incredibly good luck or clever insight.

They had no paper trail linking Mr. London to Mr. Shaw.

They had no recorded conversations.

The payoffs to Mr. London were in currency. That a lot of money floats around in Mr. Shaw's business is no big deal. He's a jeweler and will frequently pay customers in cash for items they want to sell. I am confident he gets paid in cash often. He deals with lots of cash. There would be no way to trace cash flows in his business and link them to Mr. London.

What did the feds have before the sting?

All they had to support the case was Mr. Shaw verbally blaming a friend who happened to be a partner in a Big 4 firm.

Yea, right, the feds were likely thinking.

When you think about it from that direction, there's no way the feds could have brought a criminal indictment against Mr. London without the sting.

I doubt they could have brought a successful civil charge.

I can picture what the SEC was thinking early on. If they brought a case, the target could simply deny it, and the SEC would have to drop their case because they wouldn't be able to prove anything.

Who would a jury believe? A jeweler trying to avoid a civil charge or a trusted Big 4 CPA with absolutely no blemishes on his record and absolutely no links to the trading other that shared golf tee times.

Picture this as the basis for debate in the jury room: flat-out denials from the accused combined with a complete lack of any physical, financial, or electronic evidence whatsoever. How well would that go for the feds?

Comments from Scott London interview – part 4
7/14/14

This is the fourth in a series of posts describing comments in an interview of Scott London during a four-hour CPE session on June 26.

The worst day of his life

The FBI knocked on the door of the London home at 8 AM after everyone else had left the house. Mr. London said that was the worst day of his life.

No kidding.

The interview lasted about 15 minutes. Their biggest concern? How many other people were involved.

Mr. London confessed to passing inside information and adamantly insisted he was the only person involved at the firm and had only passed information to Mr. Shaw.

The interviewing agent agreed with Mr. London's comment that it would be a good idea to get an attorney.

Mr. London obtained legal counsel the next day and called the FBI a day or two later to set up a meeting.

It took about 10 days to get the schedules together for him and his attorney to meet with the FBI, SEC, and Department of Justice.

Mr. London, with his attorney, had a two-hour meeting with all of the feds. He convinced them that the only people involved were Mr. Shaw and himself.

At some point after the big meeting (I'm not sure if it was that day or a few days later) the feds told Mr. London he could tell his firm. Prior to this, the FBI had told him not to talk to anyone at the firm about it. The reason is they weren't sure who else was involved.

At four o'clock the next day, Mr. London called to explain the situation to someone in New York; I didn't catch the name or title. Mr. London then called the local managing partner to fill him in. Those were both short discussions.

The next morning, a Friday, Mr. London received a 6 a.m. call from KPMG's in-firm legal counsel asking for contact info of his attorney. Later that day Mr. London was terminated.

Comments from Scott London interview – part 5 – motivation
7/16/14

This is the fifth in a series of posts describing comments in an interview of Scott London during a four-hour CPE session on June 26.

Motivation

In the interview, Mr. London said he is still working through the issues that led him to do this. The underlying factor is a behavioral issue inside of him. He insisted it has nothing to do with the KPMG system.

At the point that sharing transitioned from public to nonpublic information, Mr. London thinks he was responding to the appeal of human nature to help a friend in need once in a while. There was a definite slippery slope. In the midst of these comments Mr. London was clear that he took the blame.

Mr. London was asked what was going through his mind during the time his passing nonpublic information. Mr. London indicated he knew it was wrong but it didn't rise to the level of something that actually changed his behavior. He did not focus on the risk. Even now is not sure why. Possibly it is because the dollar amounts involved were small and he didn't think he would get caught.

As an aside, this is consistent with a comment in the criminal complaint that Mr. Shaw said Mr. London said in July 2012 after Fidelity closed Mr. Shaw's account. Mr. Shaw claims the comment was that insider trading is like counting cards in Las Vegas. They can't prove you did it so they will only ask you to leave the casino.

Back to the interview.

Mr. London indicates that he was under a lot of pressure at the time. He said if you're going through an adverse situation you need to consider whether that's leading you to do something wrong in a different area. Lots of pressure in one area of your life can create impaired judgment in another area of your life. You could make poor decisions as a result.

It is important to note that even though there were a number of comments trying to share ideas about motivation and thought process, at no point did Mr. London suggest any of the blame belongs anywhere other than himself. In the context of an interview there will obviously be questions to probe motivation and why this was done. Answering the questions put to him doesn't take away from the large number of times he took full responsibility for what happened.

He indicated there were warning flags in his work life, but declined to give details during the interview.

He came back to that point and said there was something going on between him and leadership at the time.

Mr. London did volunteer he has spent three or five sessions with a psychologist with each session lasting two hours. He went through a 500 question personality quiz. He shared that the results indicate he did not do this for greed. The quiz did identify some personality flaws, but he did not share what those were. He did volunteer that perhaps there were some burnout and tenure issues. I'm not quite sure what that means.

By the way, I would never, ever share the results of any such personality test with anyone, nor share I was going through counseling to sort through why I had done something foolish. Mr. London is quite brave to have shared as much as he did.

These comments are consistent with what was mentioned in an interview with Walter Pavlo: _FMR KPMG Partner Scott London Shares Cautionary Tale Before Prison_. In that interview Mr. London attributes the failure to two factors. The desire to help a friend and long tenure. He was in one position for too long. (http://goo.gl/7m0e64)

The irony to me, looking in from the outside, is that he was in the dream position of a lifetime for most CPAs who work in the audit area. Ask the technicians you know if they wouldn't eat up every second of time working as the regional audit PIC. For tons of CPAs, life couldn't get any better than that.

For someone who enjoys auditing, that would be the most wonderful job imaginable. For those of you who loooove tax – think what it would be like to sit in the office of the regional tax PIC.

The editor over at Going Concern raised the idea of self-sabotage. (**Update**: quote added for book.) (http://goo.gl/YhFJWr)

"When he started hating his job and hating his life yet no one listened to his pleas for a break, perhaps a little self-sabotage came into play:"

I don't know about that, but it is something to think about.

Comments from Scott London interview – part 6
7/21/14

This is the sixth in a series of posts describing comments in an interview of Scott London during a four-hour CPE session on June 26. The course was presented by The Pros and The Cons.

(http://goo.gl/ZOJqVO or www.theprosandthecons.com)

This post will cover a few stray comments in the interview.

Expectation of total amount of insider trading gains

As I mentioned earlier, Mr. London thinks he received around $50,000 total consisting of a combination of cash, concert tickets, and the watch which he thinks is worth perhaps $3000. If I misunderstood one or two key words in that comment and he thinks the amount is actually $70,000 total, it doesn't change the key point. I think the key phrase indicated he thought the total was $50K.

Mr. London said he was told by Mr. Shaw that the payments would be one-third of the gains. Seems to me that would be a reasonable way to split the loot – one-third for taxes and one-third to each of them.

That would reasonably have led Mr. London to think that the total gains by Mr. Shaw were the range of $150,000 to perhaps $210,000.

That would explain his professed shock at finding the total gains were actually well over $1 million.

In his own defense

Several times Mr. London referred back to his quick confession and full cooperation.

He referred to multiple mea culpa comments already made in the interview and then said he thought his core personality came through by confessing immediately when confronted.

He contrasted this with baseball players who are accused of steroid use but deny it for months or years after everyone knows they did it.

Later in the interview he came back to this idea again pointing out he did the right thing by confessing. He realizes he has tainted the entire profession and the impact would have been even worse if he denied it and caused a long investigation.

He has a good point there. If the investigation had dragged out a few weeks with daily dribbles of news hitting the NYT and WSJ, along with rumors about a dozen other companies, the damage would have been severe.

Sentencing

Going into the sentencing, his attorney argued for 6 months incarceration with a request for home confinement. Mr. London says he knew it was a pipe dream to avoid jail.

While the judge was talking at sentencing, Mr. London was guessing the judge was thinking about 3 years. As the judge starting describing mitigating factors, Mr. London figured it would be much less than 3.

He perceives that the quick confession and full cooperation was a major factor in bringing down the sentence. Without that, the sentence would have been much longer.

Other consequences

When asked about his capital account, Mr. London indicated he has a confidentiality agreement and cannot discuss it.

A stray comment by his attorney in front of a camera makes me think that his capital account was closed as a settlement with KPMG.

He thinks his pension should be covered under ERISA and therefore he hopes it will be accessible to him later on.

Comments from Scott London interview – 7th and final part
7/23/14

Preparation for prison and life after release.

This is the last post describing Scott London's interview during a four-hour CPE session on June 26. The course was presented by The Pros and The Cons. (http://goo.gl/ZOJqVO or www.theprosandthecons.com)

This post will cover preparation for prison, life afterwards, and another earned consequence.

Preparation for prison

When asked, Mr. London said he is spending a lot of time with family and friends before he reports to prison.

He has spent time talking to people whose business is coaching people to prepare for incarceration. He laughed and said who knew there was such a niche industry.

He is also getting his family ready for his absence.

I can picture what that would look like. Typically husbands and wives split the household duties. Since he is a CPA, I am guessing he took care of the family's finances. Think of all the things he needs to coach his wife on.

Explaining what to expect for the contracts that only appear once a year such as all the different insurance policies, the home warranty, safe deposit boxes, and all the other little things that go into a modern life. Writing down passwords and account numbers to all the online places.

Showing her how to do things like replace the filter on the furnace and replace the a/c fuses if they blow.

He said he is reasonably well prepared.

Life after prison

He indicated he is 51 now and will be 52 when released. He is too young to retire. He has lost his license for at least three years and thinks he can reapply after that point.

As an aside, I hope he doesn't get his hopes up too high about getting his license back.

He knows he won't be working in any financial capacity for any company registered with the SEC.

He says he still has lots of things he can do. He has expertise in human resources, technical accounting, managing people, and mentoring.

He again made a comment he has been quoted as making in public before: he will do what it takes to provide for his family.

Smart aleck commenters over at Going Concern suggest he will hit the speaker circuit and make a fortune. I mention that just to make note of their predictions.

Let's ponder that for a moment – replacing a $650K (his public comments) or $900K (various speculation) salary would require a lot of speeches. Let's assume $3k or $5K each speech. That would be somewhere between 130 (650k/5k) and 300 (900k/3k) speeches a year. In a 50 week year, that would be an average of between 2.6 and 6 speeches a week. Not likely.

Other consequence – loss of colleagues

Mr. London indicated he was a key mentor to coach and build up ten or a dozen people who moved into partnership. All those relationships went away in one day, he said.

Imagine the professional joy you would feel from having taken fifty or a hundred professionals under your wing and investing in them to the point that helped a dozen of them grow into Big 4 partners. In addition to all the other things you have done for the firm, you have grown staff to be the present and future leaders of the firm. That would produce deep pride of accomplishment in any CPA.

Now imagine never again being able to talk to those dozen people because they are under explicit instruction to not have any contact with you.

Add that to the list of hard-earned and well-deserved consequences.

About the Author

James L. Ulvog has over 25 years experience as a CPA. Since 1989, he has focused on working in the religious nonprofit environment providing audits, reviews, and consulting services. Since 2002, he has run his own accounting firm in Alta Loma, California, and is intentionally a one-person office. Most of his experience is working with small- to medium-sized organizations.

Mr. Ulvog is blogging at several sites on different topics. You can visit his weblogs at:

- Nonprofit Update (nonprofitupdate.info) - addressing issues of interest to the nonprofit community
- Attestation Update (attestationupdate.com) - issues of interest to CPAs and accountants
- Outrun Change (outrunchange.com) - trying to cope with the overwhelming change surrounding all of us

Prior to starting his own firm, Mr. Ulvog worked for a national CPA firm known for its focus on the nonprofit community. His earliest CPA experience was with two international firms: Arthur Andersen and Peat, Marwick, Mitchell.

He currently leads an adult Bible study. He serves as an elder at his church. He served on the board of a local nonprofit organization for 11 years.

Other books by this author

Tragedy of Fraud - The Ripple Effects from Fraud and the Wages Earned

There are tragic consequences from fraud that spread out to harm innocent bystanders. The perpetrator draws a wide range of well-deserved wages that will be paid in full.

The book looks at two fraud incidents to learn what happens after a fraud is discovered. One took place in a local megachurch and the other in the mayor's office of a small city.

This book is a compilation of previously published blogs posts.

Major sections of the book:

- Tragedy of Fraud – The ripple effects from the embezzlement fraud in a local church.
- Wages of Fraud – Consequences from the corruption fraud in a mayor's office.
- Why is it Difficult to Find Fraud? – The lack of documentation inside an organization makes it even more difficult to identify a fraud scheme.
- The Fraud Triangle – A discussion of the three sides of a fraud triangle. That's the idea that three components need to be present for a fraud to take place – opportunity, motivation, and rationalization. Great danger is in play when all three factors are present.

Audit. Review. Compilation. What's the difference?

What's the difference between getting an audit, review, or compilation from your CPA firm? This short, 29 page book will help you understand.

Your CPA firm could provide one of several levels of services when you hired them to look at your financial statements and issue a report. They could perform an audit, or a review, or a compilation.

There won't be big visual differences in the report they issue but there will be huge differences in cost. The reason you get the CPA's involvement in the first place is to communicate your financial information to outside parties.

There is a big difference in the comfort level those outsiders get from reading the CPA's report.

Three illustrations help explain the differences:

A football game - how does advancing to the 10-yard line compare to an audit? What would a review look like in a football game?

Buying a used car - how does taking the car for a test drive compare to a review?

Filling a bucket - How filling it up to three different levels illustrates the three levels of service.

Step Up to the Next Level:
A Guide for Local Churches to Improve Their
Internal Operations and Prepare for an Audit

Written specifically for local churches, this primer will help you step up to the basic level of internal controls and procedures every church should have. It describes key information on the audit process to help your church step up to the level of getting a financial review or audit.

Key topics:
- Why bother putting good procedures in place? (Hint: the rules have changed.)
- Fundamental financial procedures.
- How internal controls protect your staff.
- Basic internal controls that can be easily developed.
- Overview of what the audit process looks like, including recent changes you will hear about as you move into an audit.

Whatever controls your church has in place, this guide will help you step up to the next level of accountability.

Once Upon Internal Control -
A tale of good and bad ways to implement
internal controls in a local church

This is a fable of two churches

...One Church ignores internal procedures and pays a steep price.

...Another implements good procedures and can focus on mission.

This fable of two churches shows how the quality of internal controls can either prevent bad things from happening, as is the case in Southside Community Church, or allow them to take place undetected, which is the sad story at Northside. Lessons learned from each church are discussed after the story of their experiences. This short book illustrates some very simple and basic procedures you can put in place in any local church. Many small churches need to implement the controls illustrated here.

The more internal controls you can put in place, the more protection you will provide for your church, your pastor, and your staff. If you are in any position of responsibility in the financial area, these controls can help protect you.

This fable is only 9 pages long, so it is a very quick read. It would be a good introduction to internal control for your board or pastoral staff.

The ideas described would also apply to other nonprofit organizations. They can carry across to small businesses as well.

For more information on these and other books, along with information on where to find them, visit the website of the publisher of this book: Riverstone Finance Press at www.riverstonefinancepress.com.

www.ingramcontent.com/pod-product-compliance
Lightning Source LLC
Chambersburg PA
CBHW060625210326
41520CB00010B/1479